Wilhelm Kaltenborn

A forgotten past

The historical roots of the mandatory affiliation of german cooperatives to auditing federations *'Anschlusszwang'*

HEINRICH-KAUFMANN-STIFTUNG

Published by Heinrich-Kaufmann-Stiftung
des Zentralverbandes deutscher Konsumgenossenschaften e.V.
Besenbinderhof 60, 20097 Hamburg, Telefon 040 - 2800 3050
www.kaufmann-stiftung.de

Translation: Joanna Langworthy-Durier

Editing: Uta G. Barth

Composition and layout: Silke Wolf, Hamburg

Manufactured and published by: BoD - Books on Demand,
Norderstedt

2015

ISBN 978-3-73-921503-7

Table of content

The issue in question

I published a book entitled "Schein und Wirklichkeit"[1] in May 2014 which examined the existing system of cooperatives in Germany, aspects of which I was very critical of (see Kaltenborn 2014: passim). This critical examination was motivated by the fact that I have had great consideration for cooperatives for decades. I find that the German cooperative system, on the other hand, demonstrates a succession of peculiarities and contradictions which are so numerous and so serious that it was not particularly difficult, although it was time-consuming, to fill a whole book with them. One of the central points of my criticism is the statutory obligation of (registered) cooperatives to be affiliated to an auditing federation. Apart from the fact that I am fundamentally averse to forced obligations, my hostility was considerably exacerbated by the historical roots of this statutory enforced affiliation. It is namely the result of an amendment to the German Cooperative Societies Act dated October 1934, in other words 21 months after the National Socialists came to power. This amendment was part of the overall Gleichschaltung[2] and repression of cooperative systems by National Socialist authorities. After 1945, there was no public examination of the National Socialist past of cooperative federations. Indeed nothing happened, other than the invention of a few stories, spreading the idea that the cooperative system had not been tainted in any way, not even by the law of October 1934, signed by Adolf Hitler as Führer and Reichskanzler. And finally, what is seen by cooperative federations as being a positive effect of Anschlusszwang, namely protection from insolvency, can in fact also be achieved by other means.

---

1   *Appearance and Reality*
2   *Political synchronisation*

The passages from my book which deal with the origin of Anschlusszwang, the destruction of cooperative identity under National Socialist rule and the story fabricated by the official cooperative system have been summarised, revised and added to in the present publication. I would particularly like to thank Burchard Bösche here for his valuable additional contributions.

Origins of the modern cooperative movement

It is first necessary to make a few remarks about the historical origin of modern cooperatives in Germany and their original aims. Cooperative organisational structures date back to ancient times and can be found in many, if not all cultures throughout the world, in a wide variety of forms. The history of modern cooperatives begins in Germany with a man named Hermann Schulze-Delitzsch, who remains a renowned figure today. I should add that as I have long acquired the habit of referring to him as Schulze instead of Schulze-Delitzsch, I will continue to do so here. He was born Hermann Schulze in 1808 in the town of Delitzsch, which became part of Prussia as of 1815 (it was previously and is today once again part of Saxony), and his name never officially changed. He himself used the double-barrelled version in public life – particularly for his publications – as of the 1850s. However, even in Friedrich Thorwart and Philipp Stein's portrayal of his life and work – a quasi-official biography –in the final fifth volume of Schulze's writings and speeches, he is referred to throughout as Schulze (see Thorwart 1913: passim).

Schulze, member of the Prussian National Assembly which came into being after the revolution of 1848, a firm democrat, co-founder of the liberal Progressive Party in Prussia and leading national politician, founded two cooperatives in his home town of Delitzsch, a direct form of which still exist today. These were so-called raw materials associations (one for carpenters and one for shoemakers), in other words purchasing cooperatives. Many similar associations quickly sprang up all over Germany, including in the Habsburg Monarchy which was part of the German Confederation at that time. Credit associations, the forerunners of today's Volksbanks, were of significant importance in this movement. Schulze developed a theoretical concept with the founding of these cooperatives. He saw cooperatives as a – small – part of a comprehensive socio-political reform programme with which he aimed to achieve nothing less than a solution to social issues. His concept also included the founding of trade unions, called "trade associations" until 1933, and which later held the biggest strike in German history at that time in the Waldenburg coal mining district in Silesia in the winter of 1869/1870. As a parliamentarian, he resolutely fought for the freedom of association of workers - and was ultimately successful.

The main principle behind Schulze's solution to social issues was self-help. He also saw this as an indispensable doctrine for cooperative associations. He resolutely rejected state assistance, unless necessary, for example, in the event of natural disasters. For Schulze, self-help also entailed the unlimited liability of cooperative members. He called cooperatives "schools of democracy" as they were also to be used as a means of exercising self-management within municipalities and the state. The – at that time largely authoritarian – state was not to have any role. These views arose from Schulze's fundamentally democratic and liberal convictions. The voluntary nature of cooperatives was another of Schulze's unconditional principles, observed by all those that followed him in the cooperative movement, even Raiffeisen. There was no room for forced obligation in cooperative life (see Kaltenborn 2012a and 2012b: passim).

Friedrich Wilhelm Raiffeisen is another name linked to the development of modern cooperatives. He attempted to overcome rural misery by founding associations under his own concept. As mayor of a village in Westerwald, he began experimenting with different institutional models from 1847 onwards, finally developing his own cooperative concept. He too was fundamentally committed to self-help, however in a somewhat modified form. As Raiffeisen, unlike Schulze, was driven by a resolutely Christian outlook, the more prosperous could and were expected to be more widely involved in his associations than the poor. Raiffeisen was, however, even more uncompromising on the matter of the unlimited liability of cooperative members than Schulze (see Kaltenborn 2014: 40 et seq).

The Cooperative Societies Act and its development

Around ten years after the first cooperative associations were founded by Schulze in Delitzsch, the question of a satisfactory legal status for the new entities arose more and more frequently due to the movement's subsequent growth. The forms available under the (Prussian) legal system were unsatisfactory. The first was that of private association. This did not satisfy Schulze, not even in any of its subforms, primarily "because the legislator had thought of all of the possible purposes with the sole exclusion of 'business activities' (my emphasis) which is precisely the characteristic feature of the cooperative [...]". The other available legal form, the "Societät des Römisch-Deutschen Privatrechts"[3] was also insufficient, as membership changes were virtually impossible or only possible under the most cumbersome and onerous conditions. For Schulze, however, continual changes in membership were indispensable for a cooperative (see Schulze-Delitzsch 1870a: 258).

A new specific form therefore had to be created. Schulze introduced his first corresponding bill as early as 1859. The bill consisted of just five paragraphs. It, however, quickly became superfluous as the Allgemeine Deutsche Handelsgesetzbuch[4], passed by the German National Assembly of 1848/1849 in Frankfurt and gradually adapted by the individual German states, also came into force in Prussia in 1861. It then became necessary to check whether or not and to what extent the legal forms available under the commercial code would be sufficient for cooperatives. They proved to be insufficient in Schulze's opinion (see Schulze-Delitzsch 1870b: 260 et seq). A new bill therefore had to be drafted.

Schulze became a member of the Prussian House of Representatives, the second chamber of state parliament, after a by-election in 1861. In March 1863, he introduced his bill, signed by 88 other representatives (all belonging to the German Progressive Parry, the left-wing liberal party co-founded by Schulze). It was deliberated and amended in the relevant committee (committees were called commissions in the Prussian House of Representatives) and in the first chamber, the non-elected House of Lords; there was a strongly amended counter-bill from the Prussian government, followed by renewed deliberations both in the respective commission and in the House of Lords and in a plenary session of the House of Representatives. The bill was

---

3   *Society under Romano-Germanic civil law*
4   *German General Commercial Code*

8

then passed and came into force in 1867. After the founding of the German Reich in 1871, it became a Reichsgesetz[5] in virtually identical form. Reichsgesetz (see Prussian State Parliament 1863, Cooperative Societies Act (GenG) 1867 and Cooperative Societies Act (GenG) 1871).

Certain provisions of the Act differed from Schulze's original intentions in points he considered essential. Here are just two examples: according to the Act, the articles of association had to include "terms and conditions of voting rights", whereby cumulative voting was authorised (§ 3). However in the event that there was no such provision in the articles of association, each member was to be granted one vote (§ 9). This provision did not correspond at all with Schulze's vision of cooperatives, which is why he saw it as being superfluous. He was firmly convinced that this option would be completely unacceptable to true cooperatives. They would never use cumulative voting. Secondly: profit or loss was to be evenly distributed per capita - according to the Act – unless otherwise specified in the articles of association (§ 8). Schulze's bill proposed that profit and loss was to be distributed "per capita" without restriction (§ 9). The indispensable joint and several liability intended by Schulze was provided for in § 11 of the Act. (See Parisius 1868: passim and Cooperative Societies Act (GenG) 1867: passim).

The final Act therefore differed from Schulze's vision in several essential points. It seems that the 'Law of Struck', an expression coined by the former Chairman of the SPD parliamentary group Peter Struck describing how no bill comes out of Parliament in the form in which it was introduced, already applied 150 years ago. It can therefore only really be referred to as 'Schulze's Law' to a limited degree. Schulze initiated the bill and fought for it

---

with tooth and nail. He did however have to make compromises. The Act also underwent further amendments in the years that followed its enactment. They are however irrelevant here.

Schulze published a good one hundred pages in 1883, the year of his death, presenting his thoughts on a revision of the existing Cooperative Societies Act. He believed, for example, that insurance companies should not be allowed to form cooperatives. There had been previous attempts by insurance companies to form associations against Schulze's will. However, as they were subject to state supervision, they would have represented an alien presence within the cooperative system. For Schulze, it was of vital importance that cooperatives were kept as independent as possible of the state. How else could they be "schools of democracy" in a still largely authoritarian state? With regard to the auditing of cooperatives, Schulze called for a provision under which a super-audit would be carried out every two to three years by an expert auditor. This provision was intended to counter another motion to amend the Act in the Reichstag, under the terms of which local authorities would be granted a right of supervision. Schulze wanted to prevent this at all costs (see Schulze-Delitzsch 1883a: passim).

Schulze was by now slightly more open to the additional authorisation of cooperatives with limited liability. He was, however, firmly opposed to liability being limited solely to business shares but he now considered a limited guarantee to be possible. That would mean that the articles of association would have to stipulate a certain minimum liable capital. Schulze was, however, firmly convinced, or at least clearly expressed the conviction that *"the large majority of cooperatives* (would) still continue to abide by the established concept of unlimited liability". This would prevent creditors from being able to access the assets of *individual, selected* members (see Schulze-Delitzsch 1883a: 68).

This publication can be seen as Schulze's political testament on cooperatives. In this essay (which appeared posthumously in the same year as his death), he continues to assign cooperatives a central social role within the comprehensive movement to solve social issues (see Schulze-Delitzsch 1883b: passim). However, the movement's social and legal developments took different paths after Schulze's death. There were lively debates and deliberations on a revision of the Cooperative Societies Act, involving various political groups. The Act was then revised in 1889, featuring several provisions which far exceeded the previous regulations.

The revision process led to an important reform which was given a separate clause containing 12 paragraphs and included the following regulations: auditing of a cooperative had to be carried out at least once every two years by an expert auditor (§ 51), who was to be appointed by a court at the cooperative's request (§ 59). The "higher administrative authority", however, had to give its prior approval (§ 59). This destroyed an essential pillar of Schulze's cooperative structure. He had always campaigned to keep state authorities out the cooperative movement. If a cooperative belonged to a federation (which had to fulfil certain criteria), the latter had to appoint the auditor (§ 52). The federation's right to appoint auditors was to be approved by the state (§ 55). This also blatantly contradicted Schulze's intentions. The statutes of the federation were to be submitted both to courts and the higher administrative authority (§ 56). The purpose of the federation had to be "the auditing of affiliated cooperatives" and it could also pursue "the common preservation of its interests as described in § 1, particularly mutual business relationships" (§ 53). (See Cooperative Societies Act (GenG) 1889).

This Act therefore introduced federations into the life and work of cooperatives. Cooperative membership of federations was, however, still optional. These new provisions were the source of heated controversy. Schulze's friend, Ludolf Parisius, who was the first legal commentator on the Cooperative Societies Act, reported "Cooperative associations have declared their firm opposition to the bill's suggestions. The General Congress in Erfurt may have declared itself in favour of the fact that the Act will oblige cooperatives to submit their institutions and management to audit by an expert auditor at least once every three years, but it considered the remaining suggestions in this clause of the bill to be incompatible with the principles of self-help." (Parisius 1889: XXII).

Schulze's successor as 'Legal counsellor' to the General Federation, Friedrich Schenck, spoke in the Reichstag several times and in great detail on the bill relating to the Cooperative Societies Act. He was quite plain in his strong criticism of those provisions relating to federations which proposed state supervision including granting of the right to audit. He declared, "Gentlemen, the enforcement of these provisions would undoubtedly seriously damage cooperatives; these provisions are intolerable in view of the fact that cooperatives are free private associations. These provisions, should they become law, would impair the auditing institutions in place in existing cooperatives and would therefore cause serious prejudice to cooperative development, and they would ultimately pass a responsibility on to the state which the state is absolutely unable to assume." An "auditing institution with its beneficial consequences can only exist and prosper on the grounds on which it was created, on the grounds of free self-determination of cooperatives. Gentlemen, *the cooperative which has freely submitted to auditing, which freely selects the man to whom it wishes to entrust the auditing of its business management, will also happily provide the auditor it selected itself with all the necessary information he requires to obtain an accurate picture of the business dealings and give the cooperative the correct advice, and this cooperative will then be prepared to follow the auditor's sugges-tions and recommendations."* (my emphasis). Schenck added: "Our cooperatives are private commercial societies, which were only founded for the purpose of furthering the purchasing power and economic activity of its members. Forcing these associations to have their business audited by an external person represents an unprecedented interference in private law; such a provision must therefore have a most detrimental effect on the development of cooperatives". (RT 1888)

It remains to be said that cooperative federations were mas-sively opposed to the definition of their role by the Cooperative Societies Act. They saw it as endangering the principle of self-help which was one of the founding principles of the cooperative movement. Intensive discussions and fierce agitation followed within the cooperative movement (of the Schulze tradition). Many cooperatives left their own movement and changed into joint stock companies. Friedrich Thorwart, who later published the collection of Schulze's writings and speeches, wrote in the federation journal "Due to the general feeling of mistrust, it is of no surprise that the question is now being raised here and there as to whether it would not be better to renounce the cooperative form and change into a joint stock company whose business activ-ities are a lot less restricted and which are not subject to auditing by the state." (Thorwart 1889: 165/166). Another of the journal's authors commented "The number of cooperatives changing into joint stock companies is by no means minimal and there seems to be no end to this trend in sight." (Bernhardt 1889: 486/487).

Numerous amendments were also made to the Cooperative Societies Act after 1889 but they are irrelevant here. After the National Socialists came to power on 30 January 1933, several in-itial amendments were made to the Cooperative Societies Act of a rather technical nature. An amendment with serious consequences however followed in October 1934 and is at centre of this publication. A whole series of further provisions aiming to achieve even tighter control over the German economy including cooperatives were introduced in the years the followed. Consumer cooperatives were also gradually destroyed. After the war, these provisions were partially lifted again or at least modified in the Federal Republic of Germany.

The development of federations

The first cooperative federation was founded in Weimar in 1859. It was Schulze who called for a convention of those cooperatives founded according to his concept. The word 'association' was still frequently used at this time – even by Schulze himself – when speaking of cooperatives. The Cooperative Societies Act did not yet exist – this task still awaited Schulze – and the 'association' was the legal form available.

At Schulze's suggestion, 32 of these associations therefore founded their federation in the middle of June 1859, under the rather cumbersome name of 'Central-Correspondenz-Bureau der deutschen Vorschuß- und Creditvereine'⁶. This federation initially only concerned credit associations, the forerunners of today's Volksbanks. It was to develop mutual business relationships, organise the exchange of knowledge and enable "understanding in the pursuit of common interests". Schulze carried out the work in this correspondence office alone, and even without payment at first. He however very quickly received a salary for this task which occupied him full time.

---

6   *Central Correspondence Bureau of the German Credit Association*

The federation changed its name several years later. The cooperative organisation was now called 'Allgemeiner Verband der auf Selbsthülfe beruhenden deutschen Erwerbs- und Wirthschaftsgenossenschaften'[7]. The elected Director had the title 'Legal Counsellor to German Cooperatives'; he was attributed an official office. There were federal and regional sub-federations. Their directors formed the 'select committee', what we could call the Administrative Board today. Everything was regulated by the statutes of the federation and the rules of internal procedure voted by the congress, the name given to the annual meeting of members of the federation (see Schulze-Delitzsch 1870c: 101 et seq).

After Schulze's death in 1883, Friedrich Schenck succeeded him to the post of 'Legal Counsellor' to the Federation. As of this same year, Schenk – like Schulze before him – became a member of parliament, until 1893. He was also a member of the German Progressive Party and even represented the same constituency, Wiesbaden-Rheingau. Later – in 1901 – a certain Karl Korthaus founded the 'Hauptverband deutscher gewerblicher Genossenschaften'[8]. Its members were mainly craft cooperatives, who did not accept the General Federation's strict rejection of any state support, in the true tradition of Schulze (see Faust 1977: 279 et seq). Two years later, most consumer cooperatives broke away from the General Federation and founded the 'Zentralverband deutscher Konsumvereine'[9]. It was close to the social democratic workers movement and grouped around 600 consumer cooperatives when founded. (see Kaufmann 1903: passim). The 'Reichsverband deutscher Konsumvereine'[10] was formed ten

---

7   *General Federation of German Purchasing and Trading Cooperatives based on Self-Help*
8   *Federation of German Trade Cooperatives*
9   *Central Federation of German Consumer Associations*
10   *Reich Federation of German Consumer Associations*

years later, was allied to the Catholic social movement and was mainly present in the Rhineland region.

In the Raiffeisen movement, the organisational grouping of cooperatives had other goals and aims than with Schulze style cooperatives. Raiffeisen associations were strictly limited to their respective rural region by their initiator. Everyone within the community was informed of the economic situation of all members. This reduced the risks of the loan business for regional loan societies. However, there was no equitable distribution between individual loan society associations, some of which were short of funds whilst others had notable reserves. So after a few tentative attempts, Raiffeisen proceeded to found a cooperative bank whose members were loan society associations. This was the 'Rheinische Landwirtschaftliche Genossenschaftsbank eG' in Neuwied. It was founded in 1872 by 11 Raiffeisen cooperatives. This was in fact the first high-level cooperative: a central cooperative. Other such institutes were founded in the ensuing period. Raiffeisen finally accomplished another step towards the equitable distribution of money between regional banks by founding the 'Deutsche Landwirtschaftliche Generalbank', which was also given the legal form of a cooperative and whose members were the already existing central cooperatives (see Faust 1977: 346 et seq.).

The Cooperative Societies Act in force at this time –still the first Act of 1867 – did not provide for the formation of a cooperative from a group of cooperatives. Schulze therefore intervened against Raiffeisen's structure and the latter had to dissolve his model. He then, however, founded a new bank for centralised distribution, the 'Landwirtschaftliche Central-Darlehnskasse', in the form of a joint stock company this time, even if it had the most important characteristics of a cooperative. Raiffeisen then founded an actual federation for his cooperatives in 1887, the 'Anwaltschaftsverband ländlicher Genossenschaften'[11]. This organisation was comparable to the 'Allgemeiner Verband' and its objectives were also similar, including its economic aims. When founded, the federation had 24 members; by the time Raiffeisen died in 1888 - having managed the federation as its 'Legal Counsellor' up until this date – the organisation totalled over 400 members (see Faust 1977: 351 et seq). The 'Vereinigung der deutschen landwirtschaftlichen Genossenschaften'[12] had also been founded earlier, in 1883, after a long and complicated history. It was renamed the 'Reichsverband der deutschen landwirtschaftlichen Genossenschaften'[13] in 1903. The federation was managed by Wilhelm Haas who had initially been involved in the Raiffeisen movement. (see Faust 1977: 387 et seq).

The idea of housing cooperatives had also gradually gained ground since the end of the 1840s thanks to Victor Aimé Huber and his theoretical and practical efforts. Huber had promoted the idea of self-help even before Schulze. His relevant publication entitled "Selbsthülfe der arbeitenden Klassen"[14] appeared in 1848. However, housing cooperatives were not established in considerable numbers until the 1870s, after the founding of the German Reich. Its first federation was founded in 1896 (see Faust 1977: 515 et seq).

Schulze's 'Allgemeiner Verband' and the Korthaus Federation were reunited in 1920 under the name 'Deutscher Genossenschaftsverband e.V.'[15] (DGV). The two large federations of agricultural cooperatives united with other small federations in 1930 to form the 'Reichsverband der deutschen landwirtschaftli-

---

11   Federation of rural cooperatives
12   Association of German Agricultural Cooperatives
13   The Reich Federation of German Agricultural Cooperatives
14   Working Class Self-Help
15   German Federation of Cooperatives

chen Genossenschaften – Raiffeisen – e.V.'[16]. At the end of 1932, membership figures were as follows Raiffeisen Federation around 35,500 members, DGV around 3,200 members, Federation of Housing Cooperatives around 2,700 members, Central Federation of Consumer Associations around 1,000 members, Reich Federation of Consumer Associations around 250 members (see stat. yearbook 1933: 378). There were also a whole series of other smaller cooperative federations.

Today, there are approximately 40 cooperative auditing federations. Around a dozen of these are organised into the Bundesverband deutscher Wohnungs- und Immobilienunternehmen e.V. (GdW)[17]. The GDW groups companies from its sector regardless of their legal form. The previous organisational division of commercial and agricultural cooperatives was lifted around 40 years ago. The Deutscher Genossenschafts- und Raiffeisenverband (DGRV)[18] is today the largest cooperative organisation with its own extremely complex organisational structure. To put it simply, five large regional auditing federations are affiliated to the DGRV: the Genossenschaftsverband Bayern (for Bavaria), the Baden-Württembergischer Genossenschaftsverband (for Baden-Wurttemberg), the Rheinisch-Westfälischer Genossenschaftsverband (for North-Rhine Westphalia), the Genossenschaftsverband Weser-Ems (for Weser-Ems in Lower Saxony) and the Genossenschaftsverband e.V. which despite its modest and very vague name is the organisation which covers the largest geographical area. Four federal associations are also members of the DGRV: the Bundesverband der deutschen Volksbanken und Raiffeisenbanken (BVR), the Deutscher Raiffeisenverband (drv), the Mittelstandsverbund ZGV to which non-cooperative busi-

---

16   *Reich Federation of German Agricultural Cooperatives - Raiffeisen*
17   *The Federal association of German housing and real estate companies*
18   *The German Cooperative and Raiffeisen Confederation*

ness corporations are also affiliated, and the smallest of them all, the Zentralverband deutscher Konsumgenossenschaften (ZdK) which unites cooperatives from all sectors. Finally the twelve small auditing federations which are not members of the DGRV must also be mentioned. They total just a few hundred, maximum perhaps a thousand, member cooperatives. The number of housing cooperatives is indicated as 1,900. Just under 5,700 cooperatives belong to the DGRV, including around 1,100 credit institutes, more than 2,300 rural cooperatives, just under 2,500 commercial cooperatives and no more than 30 consumer cooperatives. All in all, there are around 8,000 cooperatives in Germany, totally 21.5 million members (dual membership included). Cooperative credit institutes alone total around 17.3 million members, housing cooperatives 2.8 million, rural and commercial cooperatives each have 0.5 million and consumer cooperatives 0.3 million members. (See Stappel 2013: 40).

Anschlusszwang – its establishment in October 1934

The most signification provision of the Cooperative Societies Act governing the relationship between cooperatives and auditing federations can be found in § 54. It reads: "The cooperative must belong to a federation which has been granted the right to audit (auditing federation)." This regulation exists since the legislative amendment of October 1934. The logical consequence is then formulated in § 55: "The cooperative is audited by the federation to which it belongs." (Cooperative Societies Act (GenG) 1934). The mandatory affiliation of cooperatives to auditing federations has been called "Anschlusszwang" since 1934.

This term was also used as the heading for the appropriate passage in the preamble to the National Socialist's legislative amendment. It stated that as cooperatives "were not legally precluded from leaving [a federation], it could therefore avoid unpopular instructions from its auditing federation by resigning its membership and joining another auditing federation if necessary – or none at all. Federations were, on the other hand, also able to exclude cooperatives which did not comply with their instructions, thus leaving them to their own devices. The fact that cooperatives which were not affiliated to an auditing federation were audited by a court-appointed auditor was an insufficient substitute for auditing by an auditing federation." It went on to declare "A strict centralisation of the auditing of all cooperatives by relevant auditing federations is required."(Preamble to Cooperative Societies Act (GenG) 1934; my emphasis). There was no mention of avoiding insolvency or of 'Pflichtmitgliedschaft'[19] in the official preamble.

The amendment to the Cooperative Societies Act was officially adopted by the Reich Government and signed by Adolf Hitler as "Führer and Reichkanzler" and the Reich Minister of Justice Gürtner. Parliamentary involvement was no longer necessary for its enactment. Full state power had been in the hands of the National Socialist Reich Government since the Enabling Act of March 1933.

Anschlusszwang – its justification today

When justifying Anschlusszwang today, federation representatives are very insistent that it is a means of preventing the in-

---

19   *Compulsory membership*

solvency of cooperatives. When a newly founded cooperative is registered at the Court of Registry, it must already be able to provide a certificate in which the auditing federation declares – to put it simply - that the cooperative is viable. Each cooperative is then subject to regular expert auditing thanks to Anschlusszwang which will enable early detection of weaknesses and save cooperatives from insolvency. Anschlusszwang is therefore judicious and necessary. Federations, however, use the term 'Pflichtmitgliedschaft' meaning compulsory membership although this is completely ahistorical. There are, however, also very good reasons to speak of 'Zwangsmitgliedschaft', meaning enforced membership.

The term 'compulsory membership' is also used in legal commentaries on the Cooperative Societies Act. This applies – less surprisingly – primarily to the "Lang/Weidmüller" commentary which is close to the federations. The 37th edition of this commentary appeared in 2011, following an uninterrupted series of publications since the first legal commentary on the (Prussian) Cooperative Societies Act of 1867. The commentary by Schulze's friend Ludolf Parisius, published in 1868, is seen by the publishing house as the first edition of the "Lang/Weidmüller". The latest edition writes in reference to clauses 54 and 55, looking back at 1934 and the situation beforehand, (this section is edited by Otto Korte) "If cooperatives did not belong to an auditing federation, the auditor was appointed by the competent court. This court involvement had not however produced very satisfactory results overall as the auditors did not have the necessary experience in the cooperative sector; a long-term, systematic evaluation of auditing results was particularly lacking, along with the ensuing support and assistance. Cooperatives could elude expert support and auditing by auditors from cooperative auditing federations by resigning from the federation.

These conclusions and the lessons learnt from the Great Depression in the early 1930s resulted in the legislative amendment of 1934."(Lang/Weidmüller 2011: 632).

The following is also added: "This compulsory membership is based on the experience that auditing by court-appointed auditors had not proven satisfactory, that auditing can only be fully effective in conjunction with continuous support and the monitoring of audits by the same auditing federation, and that cooperatives affiliated to federations have been better able to withstand an economic crisis than other cooperatives or companies with a different legal form. This was particularly evident during the years of economic crisis before the amendment in 1934." (Lang/Weidmüller 2011: 650).

The Great Depression in the years around 1930 apparently therefore shook cooperatives non-affiliated to auditing federations to a much greater extent. Other legal commentaries on this Cooperative Societies Act tell the same story, for example Beuthien writes "After the First World War and during the Great Depression of 1930/31, it was primarily those cooperatives that did not belong to a federation which collapsed." (Beuthien 2011: 674). Hartmut Glenk gave no justification when maintaining quite succinctly in his Cooperatives Manual of 1996 that the law of 1889 had been inadequate in this respect, "as the legal regulation of 1889, according to which either a federation or a court had to appoint an auditor, proved to be unsatisfactory, the legislative amendment of 1934 transferred responsibility for auditing to the federation to which the cooperative belonged." (Glenk 1996: 265). In his second edition of 2013, under a reworded title, Glenk adheres to Lang/Weidmüller's claims that auditing federations are to be thanked for the financial resilience of cooperatives, and that other, i.e. harsher lessons had been learnt during the Great Depression. He writes "It is essentially the auditing federations that are to be thanked for the fact that the collapse of only very few cooperatives has been registered in recent years. The cooperative has proven to be the legal form most able to withstand an economic crisis" (Glenk 2013: 307). And he adds "A closer relationship with cooperative federations also seemed wise in the wake of the Great Depression." (Glenk 2013: 308).

Klaus Müller was a bit more critical of the usual justifications in his legal commentary, "The reasons behind the introduction of compulsory membership to a cooperative federation under the amendment of the Cooperative Societies Act of 30 October 1934 (see paragraph 1) were already questionable at that time. It consisted of the belief that the economic collapse of cooperatives in the late 1920s and early 1930s was due to the cooperatives' lack of an economically adequate business organisation or inadequate management expertise, and that the integration of cooperatives into a control system with extensive powers had to be enforced. … In this economic and legal view of cooperatives, the insolvency proceedings of that time were however seen solely as a cooperative phenomenon, despite being the result of the Great Depression and other - internal – factors which affected companies of other legal forms in equal measure." (Müller 1998: 757)

Economic stability of cooperatives during the Great Depression

The reasons given today for the amendment of the Act in 1934, with the introduction of enforced membership, are, in fact, historically entirely incorrect. Müller accurately recognised this in his commentary. Let us first take a look at a few figures. The most devastating crisis years were actually the four years from the start of 1929 until the end of 1932 (see e.g. Schulze 1993: 151 and Wehler 2003: 257 et seq). Let us see how the number of cooperatives changed in Germany over this period. All figures are taken from the statistical yearbooks of the German Reich from that time. Every year they included an overview with the heading "Total number of Cooperatives (without central cooperatives)" as registered on 1 January of that year. The following figures were recorded:

1929   52,153 cooperatives (see statistical yearbook 1929: 349),

1930   52,559 (see statistical yearbook 1933: 377),

1931   52,505 (see statistical yearbook 1933: 377),

1932   52,030 (see statistical yearbook 1933: 377) and

1933   51,499 cooperatives (see statistical yearbook 1933: 377).

So their number decreased by 654 over these four years of economic crisis (although they even increased in the first year). This represents believe it or not just 1.25%.

This is a net figure. It therefore also includes the founding of new cooperatives as well as normal exits (e.g. due to fusions). Let us compare this figure with the corresponding development of companies with other legal forms now. These are once again net figures. According to the current logic of federations and the majority of legal commentators, the drop in companies with other legal forms should therefore have been even smaller. The information on joint stock companies (Aktiengesellschaften) and private limited companies (Gesellschaften mit beschränkter Haftung) is the most significant and the statistical yearbooks are able to help us once again.

Let us look at joint stock companies first: the year shifts here as the respective reference date in the statistical yearbook is 31 December, unlike for cooperatives. The currency reform of 1923 in the wake of hyperinflation resulted in an era-related particularity for joint stock companies of that time. Until the start of the

1930s, there were still joint stock companies (admittedly only a few) who still declared their shares in Mark (the name valid until the end of 1923) and not yet in Reichsmark (RM). The figures refer to the sum of both groups.

On 31 December 1928 and therefore on 1 January 1929, there were 11,842 joint stock companies (see statistical yearbook 1929: 339). Four years later, on 31 December 1932, this figure was 9,638 (see statistical yearbook 1933: 367). There was therefore a decrease of 2,204 joint stock companies. This corresponds with a drop of 18.6% compared to 1928/29. There were 680 insolvencies in this period, which represents 5.7% (see statistical yearbook 1929: 339; statistical yearbook 1930: 383; statistical yearbook 1931: 363; statistical yearbook 1932: 359; statistical yearbook 1933: 367).

It is a bit more complicated to determine figures for private limited companies. The statistical yearbooks do list the change in numbers of other legal forms, including private limited companies but the overall number of private limited companies is missing in those years. Legal literature can, however, help here, particularly large, extensive commentaries on the laws governing private limited companies whose introductory chapters also feature information on the history of private limited companies. We can therefore learn that there were 57,338 private limited companies in Germany in 1926 (Michalski 2010: 62). I assume that the reference date for this figure was the 31 December 1926. In 1927 and 1928 the number of private limited companies reduced by an overall 11,248 (see statistical yearbook 1930: 368). There were therefore still 46,090 at the turn of the year 1928/1929. This figure then dropped by 2,490 (see statistical yearbook 1930: 368) in 1929 and by a further overall 1,440 companies (see statistical yearbook 1933: 368) in the three years that followed – in other words by 3,930 over the four years of economic crisis that are of interest to us here. This represents 8.5%.

Let us now look at these figures again:

Drop in cooperatives 1.25%,
Drop in joint stock companies (AG) 18.6%,
Drop in private limited companies (GmbH) 8.5%.

The fall in the number of companies with share capital was therefore respectively 15 and 7 times greater than that of cooperatives.

Now there may be several other reasons behind this fall in joint stock companies and private limited companies other than the direct consequences of the Great Depression – an increase in fusions, for example, or relocation abroad. The legal commentary on private limited companies also names tax discriminations as a cause (see Michalski 2010: 62). However such reasons could only explain a small proportion of the drop in numbers. In conclusion, it can therefore be said that cooperatives resisted the Great Depression much better, indeed surprisingly better, than joint stock companies and private limited companies, even without Anschlusszwang. The figures alone demonstrate that the historical justification for Anschlusszwang given by cooperative federations and appropriate legal literature is a pure invention. It is not without reason that this justification did not appear anywhere in the preamble to the law of 1934.

Cooperative federations, on the other hand, saw a more depressing development over those years. The statistical yearbooks namely list federations with their membership numbers. This too is rather complicated as the federation landscape changed considerably at precisely this time. Firstly, the "Hauptverband der deutschen Baugenossenschaften"[20] as it was listed in 1928, was called "Hauptverband Deutscher Baugenossenschaften und -Gesellschaften"[21] four years later (the figure for 1932 still

---

20   *Main Federation of German Housing Cooperatives*
21   *Main Federation of German Housing Cooperatives and Companies*

however only refers to affiliated cooperatives, without housing companies of other legal forms).

The following agricultural federations existed in 1928 (with membership figures as registered at the end of that year):

Reich Federation of German Agrculturalh   26,085 Cooperatives
Cooperative Federation of German Raiffeisen 8,252 Cooperatives
Reich Regional Cooperative Federation   903
Union of cooperatives close to
German Farmers Association   1,549
A total therefore of: 36,789

(see stat. yearbook 1929: 347) rural cooperatives.

The members of all these federations were grouped into the "Reichsverband der deutschen landwirtschaftlichen Genossenschaften – Raiffeisen e.V."[22] at the end of 1932, to which the above-listed figures must be attributed for 1928.

Membership developed as follows over the four years of economic crisis:

Membership of cooperative federations	End of 1928	End of 1932
German Federation of Cooperatives	3,559	3,230 (- 9.2%)
Central Federation of German Consumer Associations	1,069	964 (- 9.8%)
Reich Federation of German Consumer Associations	27	259 (- 6.2%)
Federation of Housing cooperatives	2,680	2,667 (- 0.5%)
Agricultural federations	36,789	35,482 (- 3.6%)
Total no. of cooperatives in these federations	44,373	42,602 (- 4%)

(see stat. yearbook 1929: 347) (see stat. yearbook 1933: 378)

There were also a good number of smaller auditing federations, mostly regional, besides the above-listed federations. Their

---

22   *Raiffeisen Reich Federation of German Agricultural Cooperatives*

membership numbers are extremely difficult to establish. We can however obtain the following picture:

Total number of cooperatives

overall		in larger federations		in smaller federations or non-affiliated

Turn of the year 1928/29

| 52,153 | = | 44,373 | + | 7,780 |

Turn of the year 1932/33

| 51,499 | = | 42,602 | + | 8,897 |

Difference

| - 1.25% | | - 4.0% | + | 14.4% |

Contrary to all the stories told by cooperative federations and repeated in legal commentary on the Cooperative Societies Act, the number of cooperatives affiliated to large federations fell considerably during the four years of economic crisis, whilst the number affiliated to smaller federations or not affiliated at all ("wild cooperatives" as they were called in the 1930s) rose quite significantly. So, being a member of large established federations with expert auditors did not protect member cooperatives from financial ruin.

After October 1934, all cooperatives had to be affiliated to a federation. According to the stories told by federations and legal commentators, cooperatives were then much safer than before. But how did the figures actually change? Let us look at the years 1935 (i.e. after the regulation came into force) to 1938 - another four year period:

Total number of cooperatives (without central cooperatives) as at 31 December of each year

1934 53,348
1935 53,216
1936 52,595

1937 51,704

1938 50,940

(see statistical yearbook 1940: 468).

As we can see, the figure dropped by 2,408 over four years. This represents 4.5%. Despite the 'blessing' of the Anschlusszwang, over three and a half times more cooperatives disappeared in that period than during the four worst years of the Great Depression. Many factors which had nothing to do with Anschlusszwang may have played a role here, such as the development of a state-controlled economy in preparation for war. But this does certainly not substantiate the arguments used by federations and legal commentators.

Auditing and enforced membership: the federations' position up until 1934

Today, federations repeatedly maintain that enforced membership came about at the request of the federations of that time. This is why we first need to look at how the federations' view developed regarding the necessity to audit cooperatives. The first federation was created in 1859, initiated by Schulze. It was only in 1862, three years later (five years before the Cooperative Societies Act came into force), that a debate was held in one of the first sub-federations, that of the Middle Rhine region, on whether or not the federation should also handle its members' annual accounts. It was decided as a result that the Federation Director, Friedrich Schenck, should ensure that a "suitable expect" was available on request "to advise associations or audit their annual accounts". This was by no means intended as a form of supervision by the federation, as it saw this as being "incompatible with cooperative self-help and self-management". This also matched Schulze's vision. When the introduction of official supervision was envisaged by conservative, pro-state circles, Schulze altered his position. He ensured a resolution was passed by the Federation Congress in Kassel in 1881 under which sub-federations, in other words regional federations, were to offer the possibility of "regularly recurring audits" – naturally for member cooperatives only. This marked the birth of the auditing system for cooperatives (see Letschert 1951: 16).

In his last thoughts on an amendment to the Cooperative Societies Act, his so to say political testament on cooperatives dated 1883, Schulze clearly opposed all attempts to introduce statutory regulations on cooperative federations. "The Act can naturally neither decree nor prohibit the creation of such federations, and must, on the contrary, enable the freedom of association of its participants." It was also to adhere strictly to the cooperative principles of self-help and voluntary action (see Schulze-Delitzsch 1883a: 94/95). Schenk, Schulze's successor as 'Legal Counsellor' to the General Federation - the very same Schenk who was Director of the sub-federation for the Middle Rhine region – also took the same line, both as Member of Parliament and, as we have already seen, in his firm stance during the parliamentary debate on the law which came into force in 1889. The Act that was finally adopted enabled a choice between auditing by a federation and by a court-appointed auditor.

Cooperatives continued to go under time and again during that period. Such outcomes were naturally considered highly regrettable in the cooperative system. Federations subsequently intensified their offer of auditing services, but not a single leading federation representative suggested the idea of forcing a cooperative to join a federation. This would have strongly contradicted established cooperative principles.

A brochure on "auditing by the federation" by the Deutsche Genossenschaftsverband (DGV), which can confidently be regarded as an official brochure, states *"The 'Allgemeiner Verband' firmly opposes the granting of any statutory, compulsory authority to auditing federations*, which would naturally entail obligations for the federation. This would burden the auditing federation with a responsibility which it cannot assume; it would also inevitably lead to state supervision. It is due to these concerns that the 'Allgemeiner Verband' has always expressed its opposition to a statutory expansion of auditing, which has long been the subject of a regular campaign by influential circles. It also rejects any *state* or *municipal* supervision. … *Self-help, self-management and direct responsibility: these are the three pillars on which Schulze-Delitzsch cooperatives are built and they are viewed and advocated by the 'Allgemeine Verband' as the essential condition for any cooperative activity.* The cooperative must be free in its decisions. Self-management and direct responsibility would inevitably be undermined if an auditing federation was given statutory authority over its cooperatives." (Letschert 1921: 48/49; emphasis in the original). The author repeats these statements in another edition in 1927, the only thing that had changed was his German spelling (Letschert 1927: 101/102).

The 67th Congress of the DGV in Hamburg in 1930 adopted a comprehensive list of guiding principles on auditing, divided into 25 individual points, under the heading "Guiding principles relating to the lecture: Development and Expansion of Auditing within the DGV". There was no mention of enforced membership of any kind anywhere in the guidelines themselves or in the relevant lecture (given by the prominent cooperative leader Heinrich Bredenbreuker) (see DGV Congress 1930: 10 et seq and 167 et seq). The only idea relating to a change in statutory requirements for federation membership developed by Bredenbreuker was that of noting in the register whether a cooperative belonged to a federation or not (see DGV Congress 1930: 183). Johann Lang, member of the DGV Executive Board, had previously suggested in his report that auditing of cooperatives should be carried out once a year instead of every two years as required at the time – regardless of whether this was done by the federation auditor or by an auditor appointed by the court (see Congress 1930: 42 et seq). These were the only legal provisions requested by the Deutscher Genossenschaftsverband (DGV). These were the only provisions for statutory auditing requested by the Deutsche Genossenschaftsverband (DGV). No-one had thought of Anschlusszwang yet.

The next DGV Congress also saw no mention of the need for compulsory affiliation of cooperatives to federations. Lang only repeated his call for a legal provision stipulating annual auditing (see DGV Congress 1932: 47/48). The next congress was held the following year, 1933, i.e. after the National Socialists had come to power, and there was still no talk of Anschlusszwang – only of other contemporary issues which we will look at later.

There had indeed been efforts to strengthen auditing powers in relation to cooperatives, and therefore strengthen the influence of federations, even before the First World War. They had, however, come from outside the cooperative system. A doctoral thesis from 1936 reports "That these efforts were unsuccessful was due to the resistance of cooperative federations. They repeatedly emphasised that the cooperative system depended entirely on self-management and direct responsibility. Extending the rights of federations meant intervening in the authority of (AR), without any resulting benefits for the cooperatives." (Feldmann 1936: 80).

Discussions continued during the Weimar Republic with no change in the positions, "The question of reforming the cooperative audit system was raised frequently after the war, and the need for compulsory measures by federations and also for Anschlusszwang was also raised, particularly in the press. ... The federations did not however change their position in the face of these suggestions: mandatory measures and forced affiliation to federations were emphatically rejected." (Feldmann 1936: 81). Enforced membership was not even requested by the Reichsverband der deutschen landwirtschaftlichen Genossenschaften – Raiffeisen – e.V. until 1934, or by any other federation.

The situation in fact developed as follows: the Deutsche Zentralgenossenschaftskasse[23] (known as the 'Preußische Zentralgenossenschaftskasse'[24] until 1932) presented recommendations for tighter auditing requirements in October 1932 (see Feldmann 1936: 83). By this time, the bank had become a Reich institution by order of the Reich President. It had been founded in 1895 as a state institute of Prussia. It was to work in close cooperation with federations to provide state funds for easier loans to cooperatives. The large majority of funds went to rural cooperatives. In light of this background, the bank also felt entitled to voice its opinion on the cooperative auditing system (see Faust 1967: 28 et seq). The Zentralgenossenschaftskasse's requests for stricter auditing regulations prompted an answer from the federations, followed by the drafting of a further text as a basis for negotiations between the cooperative bank and the federations. These negotiations led to a joint proposal for discussions with government ministries. These in turn resulted in a ministerial bill. This bill was, however, then significantly modified once more - without consultation with the federations. This version was then adopted in the Act of October 1934. (See Feldmann 1936: 84 et seq). The first five drafts – representing the federation's position – "maintain the principle dis-

---

23   *German Cooperative Savings Bank*
24   *Prussian Cooperative Savings Bank*

tinction between affiliated and free cooperatives"; only the final – ministerial – text stipulates Anschlußzwang (Feldmann 1936: 89, see also: 134).

A paper written in 1972 on "cooperative support federations" observes that "Only the *last* bill presented by the Nazi Reich Ministry of Justice stipulated Anschlusszwang as was later adopted by law." The claim that it was legally prescribed in 1934 in agreement with the cooperative federations is "clearly refuted by the contents of the draft bills of the Cooperative Societies Act" (Pramann 1972: 30 et seq). The story as told by federations and legal commentators that Anschlusszwang had been necessary to protect cooperatives, which had been too susceptible to insolvency during the Great Depression in the early 1930s, has already proven to be unfounded. And now we also know that it is nothing more than a self-serving declaration (to put it mildly) to suggest today that Anschlusszwang met the wishes of the federations.

Anschlusszwang as part of the National Socialist's ruling policy

So what were the motives behind this amendment and whose were they? There are various opinions here. Müller is quite emphatic in his legal commentary, "the introduction of compulsory membership in § 54 of the Cooperative Societies Act (GenG) was not [my emphasis] to fulfil National Socialist ideology…" (Müller 1998: 757). This is also the argument used by federations. However, anyone who has had just the briefest glimpse of the political scenery of 1933/34 would find it absurd to imagine that the National Socialists, who had not hesitated to put all their energy and brutality into imposing their own vision of state and society since they had come to power on 30 January 1933, of all people, would be so accommodating to such a non-political request for Anschlusszwang from cooperative federations.

A jurisprudential thesis was submitted to the University of Hamburg in 1972 on the topic of the legal status of cooperative federations. I have already quoted several extracts. It included both a fundamental and detailed examination of the years 1934 to 1945, and in particular of the legal changes made in 1934. Its author was Götz Pramann. I have presented his most important arguments here but would like to refer readers to the original for its wealth of documents and sources (remarks on pages 29 to 47) (see Pramann 1972: 29 et seq). Pramann first looks at Anschlusszwang in relation to other legislative amendments in 1934. These primarily include a "tightening of the scope and content of auditing" and the "granting of certain powers to auditing federations for the implementation of auditing and the safeguarding of audit results".

When it comes to the principles of National Socialist policy, Pramann refers readers to the "NSDAP's declared objectives" which were to replace Roman law and its materialistic outlook with a German "Gemeinrecht"[25]. The precedence given to private law had to be surmounted. The nation was to be at the heart of law and every rule in Gemeinrecht or völkisches Recht[26] had to be in line with this ideology. Pramann explained that in practice, this resulted in an "unforeseen growth" in public law. "The private sphere was in parts considerably restricted in favour of the Gemeinschaft[27]; the large majority of rules from the Nazi period were the means for achieving this goal."

---

25   *Common law*

26   *Racial-nationalistic law*

27   *Community*

The National Socialist stance on the economy was also resolutely different to that of the previous era. It was now said that the economy had to serve the nation. The respective tenet was as follows: "Die Führung und Aufsicht der Wirtschaft dem Staat, die Verwaltung der Wirtschaft selbst"[28]. "To achieve this goal, an organisation was needed that could manage and supervise economic transactions of national economic importance. This instrument already partially existed in the form of existing economic associations and federations." Cooperatives at that time numbered around 53,000 with approx. 8 million members, and therefore had its own specific economic importance. "State control of the co-operative organisation [therefore] became an absolute necessity for the National Socialists."

The state had already acquired the means of influencing the central federations' statutes and staff appointments (there were now only four central federations by March 1934, one each for the commercial, rural, consumer and housing cooperative sectors). This was achieved by the law on the safeguarding of public utility in the housing sector of July 1933, the decree on the provisional creation of the Reichsnährstand29 of January 1934 and the law on the preparation of an organic structure of the German economy of February 1934. A "way [was therefore] found to exert influence over the sub-federations." The aim was to tighten the content and scope of auditing. "For the National Socialist State, compulsory auditing was a means of supervising economic transactions." It "primarily [served] the Volksgemeinschaft30", and not the members of the cooperatives themselves or their creditors. Auditors became "Beauftragte der Volksgemeinschaft"[31] – as in joint stock

28   *Management and supervision of the economy in the hands of the state, its administration falls on the economy itself*

29   *Reich Food Corporation*

30   *National community*

31   *official representatives of the nation*

companies. The audit certificate now also had to confirm that the "management is lawful and considered satisfactory in the interests of common good". The auditor's report therefore acquired "a certain public authority". "This official task entailing such public authority can be viewed as a special state function".

Pramann quotes Heinrich Bredenbreuker "one of the leading representatives of the cooperative organisation at that time", who we have seen earlier, as having declared at the Palatinate Federation Congress in 1936 that "auditing federations have today acquired the quality of a public institution. This is largely due to the lessons learnt from the years of economic crisis, but is also a result of the changes to the role of the economy within the National Socialist State." Rudolf Ruth, who was also active in the cooperative movement, stated in 1935 that appointing federations as auditors was "to be seen as an important asset for the National Socialist State as it offers another valuable means of achieving National Socialist economic order" (see Pramann 1972: 40 et seq).

A more recent investigation into credit cooperatives in the period between 1933 and 1945 contains compelling remarks on "the ideological background of the Führerprinzip[32] and Gleichschaltung" which is the title of a sub-heading. The author, Hermann-Josef ten Haaf, goes one step further than Pramann and starts with the ideology of race when looking at the ideological principles of National Socialist rule. "The ultimate purpose of the national state was, in Hitler's view, the preservation of 'rassische Urelemente'[33]". The individual was merely "a cog in the wheel of the nation". This "monistic view of the nation matched the vision of total identity between the rulers and the ruled". This was reflected in the Führerprinzip. (see ten Haaf 2011: 221 et seq). The Führerprinzip meant "first ensuring that the will of the Führer

---

32   *Leader principle or "Führer" principle*
33   *Pure racial elements*

Adolf Hitler was implemented, across all hierarchy." The question of how willingly this directive was adopted in parts of the cooperative movement can be answered on the basis of a passage from a credit cooperative's business report for 1933 and quoted by ten Haaf, in which it stated that that the conditions were now in place "to ensure that the leader's iron will could be enforced right through to the smallest unit in the nation". (ten Haaf 2011: 228).

Kuno Bludau wrote a paper in 1968 simply entitled "National Socialism and Cooperatives". In it he wrote "The National Socialists did not abolish existing institutions but concentrated instead on changing the core of these institutions." They took care to "encompass all areas of society". They also changed the legal basis of self-management, so "that state leaders could intervene at any time". Political education, in other words indoctrination with national socialist ideology, focussed its efforts, for example, on vocational and professional associations for craftsmen and retailers. There was no need for cooperative federations to be involved as there were numerous organisational and personal links between the two groups. Gleichschaltung was therefore achieved through "social units with any kind of connection with cooperative organisations" (see Bludau 1968: 36 et seq).

Another characteristic element of the National Socialist cooperative system was the introduction of the mandatory affiliation of auditing federations to central federations. This was included in the Act of 1934 (§ 62), and appeared almost as an obvious extra. In keeping with the Führerprinzip, the central federations had the greatest power. The appointment of publically-appointed cooperative auditors was also established at the same time (§ 63b) and then regulated by a decree in 1936. These appointments – which were also a consequence of Anschlusszwang – represented a further step towards the integration of the cooperative movement in the National Socialist State. The decree featured a total of 28 articles. (see Decree on Public Auditors (WP-Verordnung)1936).

§ 4 made provisions for an Admissions Committee consisting of three representatives from the private sector (appointed by the Reich Minister for Economic Affairs, two of whom were nominated by central cooperative federations and the third by the Reich Chamber of Commerce), three representatives from the profession (nominated by the Institute of Auditors and appointed by the Reich Minister for Economic Affairs, two of whom were appointed in consultation with the central cooperative federations), one representative from the Deutsche Zentralgenossenschaftskasse (also appointed by the Reich Minister for Economic Affairs following nomination by the bank's President). There was a Central Office for publically-appointed auditors. It was mentioned in § 21 which stated "Auditors publically-appointed according to the aforementioned conditions are monitored by the Central Office during the execution of their profession, without prejudice to the tasks of the central cooperative federations (§§ 55 et seq of the Cooperative Societies Act)." Everything was done to revoke cooperative self-determination even for those cooperative federations who were already politically synchronised and compliant.

§ 6 governed the "personal qualifications" of these auditors. They had to live in well-ordered economic circumstances, be at least 30 years of age and fulfil other similar conditions. However, the following provision was also an integral part of the cooperative auditing system: "Juden sind von der Zulassung zur Fachprüfung ausgeschlossen. Wer Jude ist, bestimmt § 5 der ersten Verordnung zum Reichsbürgergesetz vom 14 November 1935 (Reichsgesetzbl.[34] I S. 1333)."[35] And there was also finally § 14:

---

34   *National Law Gazette*

35   *Jews are not admitted to the qualifying examination. Who is a Jew is defined by § 5 of the first decree to the Reich Citizenship Law of 14 November 1935*

"Bei der Bestellung hat der Wirtschaftsprüfer folgenden Eid zu leisten: ‚Ich schwöre bei Gott, daß ich dem Führer und Reichskanzler Adolf Hitler unbedingten Gehorsam leisten werde und daß ich die Aufgaben und Pflichten eines öffentlich bestellten Wirtschaftsprüfers gewissenhaft und unparteiisch erfüllen, Verschwiegenheit bewahren und die von mir verlangten Gutachten gewissenhaft und unparteiisch erstatten werde.'[36] (Decree on Public Auditors (WP-Verordnung) 1936).

Cooperatives and their federations (if 'their' is still the right word) had acquired a highly public quality in an increasingly National Socialist State. The time of associations under private law was definitely over. The betrayal of Schulze (and also of Raiffeisen) was complete and enforced membership, the fruit of National Socialist ideology, played an essential role in all of this.

National Socialist ideology in cooperatives

It is quite remarkable how leading cooperative members adopted National Socialist ideology as their own, in some cases even before 1933 and on a more widespread basis afterwards.

There is a very comprehensive, 120 page memorandum from 1940. It appeared as a 'work report' from the 'Akademie für Deutsches Recht'[37]. This Academy was founded in 1933, in other words quite soon after the National Socialists came to power. Hans Frank, its President until 1942, was also Reich Commissioner for the Gleichschaltung of Justice in 1933 and became Reich

---

36   *Upon appointment, the auditor must make the following oath: 'I swear by God that I will offer utter obedience to the Führer and Reichskanzler Adolf Hitler, and that I will fulfil my tasks and duties as a public-appointed auditor conscientiously and impartially, exercise discretion and that I will prepare the expert reports requested of me conscientiously and impartially*
37   *Academy for German Law*

Minister without a portfolio one year later. In his letter of appointment, the Academy was described as an institution which should enable him "to participate in the implementation of the National Socialist vision in all areas of law" (Akademie für Deutsches Recht Vol. I 1986: XIII). Frank became Governor General of occupied Poland during the Second World War. He was sentenced to death at the Nuremberg trials in 1946 for crimes against humanity. The Akademie für Deutsches Recht had the task of creating a standardised, 'völkisch' law in Germany to which numerous committees were to contribute.

The Committee for Cooperative Law began its work in February 1936. Its Chairman was Walter Granzow, who had been Reich Settlement Commissioner since August 1933 and was responsible for agricultural policy in the Reich Leadership of the NSDAP until 1938. He was also second President of the Reichsverband der landwirtschaftlichen Genossenschaften. Hans Frank opened the first committee session with the following words "The Führer has entrusted the 'Akademie für Deutsches Recht' with the task of implementing the National Socialist program in all areas of law and the economy in cooperation with the relevant departments responsible for legislation. The *totalitarian claim of National Socialism,* which, when applied to the area of law, requires the *readjustment of all legal concepts in a National Socialist sense,* reveals the huge responsibility and importance of the 'Akademie für Deutsches Recht'" (Akademie für Deutsches Recht Vol. IV 1989: 71; my emphasis). The Committee Chairman, Granzow, replied "We will begin work immediately and will shortly submit proposed amendments to you to enable the integration of the cooperative system, in its full scope and range of activities, in the new state and its aims, so that it can fully participate in the great tasks which the Führer has set himself." (Akademie für Deutsches Recht IV 1989: 72).

It was in this context that the memorandum compiled by the Committee for Cooperative Law was issued in 1940, under the heading "German Cooperative Law".

It is astounding to note how just a few simple words were used to graft the National Socialist concept to the cooperative idea. In the "General Section" on the "foremost characteristics of the entire German cooperative system", it says that they are the spirit of self-help and "der Wille der Gemeinschaftsarbeit"[38] (see Frank 1940: 2). This only sounds like a moderate alteration as self-help appears to be accepted. The term 'Gemeinschaftsarbeit'(community effort - which may sound rather strange today), on the other hand, meant the implementation of National Socialist ideology. This is clear from the details on "Cooperative Federations and Auditing". These stated "The possibility given to cooperative federations to exercise centralised influence over the management of affiliated companies [through the introduction of Anschlusszwang in 1934], and to bring their business and economic policies into line with standardised concepts, is naturally of increased significance at a time which requires the utmost exertion and centralisation of all economic forces, and enables cooperatives to make a notable contribution to the great aims of the nation's economy" (see. Frank 1940: 107). There is no mention of the fact that the legislative amendment of 1934 was intended to safeguard the existence of cooperatives. Instead, federations were to orchestrate standardisation of their compulsory members. It is explicitly stated that the amendment of 1934 was "already in line with the new legislative and economic doctrine" (see Frank 1940: 111). This memorandum also repeatedly refers to 'Verbandszwang'[39]. The committee that drew these conclusions in 1940 also included Johannes Lang and Ludwig Weidmüller, the

---

38   *The spirit of community effort*
39   *Enforced membership of federations*

42

former was the Legal Counsellor, in other words President, of the DGV, the latter was its lawyer.

Together, Lang und Weidmüller, continued the legal commentary begun by Parisius in 1868. Their edition of 1938 consequently states *A new page in the history of the German Cooperative Societies Act began with the national elevation of the German people under their Führer and Reichskanzler Adolf Hitler in 1933.* National Socialist ideology was expressed in several comprehensive amendments to the Cooperative Societies Act, bearing testimony to the will of the National Socialist State to intensively enhance the German Cooperative Act" They list all of these amendments and consequently also mention the Act of October 1934, however, without any indication that this had also respected the wish of cooperative federations. At the end of their introduction, Lang and Weidmüller express their confidence that the work by the Committee for Cooperative Law at the Akademie für Deutsches Recht would *form the foundation for a final restructuring of the Cooperative Societies Act in line with National Socialist principles*". (Lang/Weidmüller 1938: 11 et seq; emphasis in the original). The explanatory text on § 54 (which introduced Anschlusszwang), also appears under the heading "Anschlusszwang" (Lang/Weidmüller 1938: 146).

Another reference is of interest to us here: Reinhold Henzler, a much-published Professor at the Institute for Cooperatives in Frankfurt am Main, wrote a number of essays after the war which appeared in the "Zeitschrift für das gesamte Genossenschaftswesen", the magazine on the theory of cooperatives by excellence. After his death, a collection of his lectures and essays were published in 1970 in a posthumous tribute (see Henzler 1970). He had however also written quite a lot before the war, for example about the Führer concept in the German cooperative system in 1934, in which he expands on the National Socialist style of cooperative thinking of that time in his own manner: "The overall interests of the cooperative community demand stability in 'Gemeinschaftsführung'40. The leaders must be able to adjust their actions to long-term goals in each individual situation. Only then can the leader of the cooperative finally demonstrate and convince cooperative members of the validity of his actions. The community must first follow him unconditionally, if necessary under force." (My emphasis). Let us remind ourselves that Schulze described cooperatives as "schools of democracy". According to Henzler, however, long-term voluntary allegiance was required in cooperatives. Direct democracy could lead to random majorities. "In view of the possible dangers described, it is in the interests of the cooperative that the Cooperative Board, which bears a formidable responsibility, is given a strong, substantiated foundation. The involvement of a higher cooperative instance, for example that entrusted with auditing, ought to be the solution. Its involvement in the appointment and dismissal of the Board – its activities were previously only audited or possibly monitored – would reinforce the (Board's) position in relation to cooperative members and businesses..." Such a regulation, involving the appointment of board members by federations, was "in line with a consistent implementation of the Führerprinzip". It is "easier to implement in the cooperative system than in the private sector and involves the cooperative organisation's wide-reaching alignment with state policy." The Supervisory Board would, however, consequently lose its importance according to Henzler (Henzler 1934: 37 et seq). This essay was not, however, included in the 1970 anthology published by the 'Zeitschrift für das gesamte Genossenschaftswesen'. The Führerprinzip was by then of course no longer topical.

---

40 *Community leadership*

For Henzler, the "introduction of the Führerprinzip throughout the German cooperative system", already in place in agricultural cooperatives, required one specific condition, namely "the corporate restructure of the entire German economy". Even before the legal provision on Anschlusszwang, Henzler wrote *"The Führer concept could already be applied to the cooperative system now if all cooperatives had to affiliate to an auditing federation* and if all auditing federations, whose activities did not cover the entire German Reich, were organised in a central cooperative federation which acted as head organisation." (Henzler 1934: 40; my emphasis).

This is clear enough: Anschlusszwang as a vehicle of the Führer concept. This goal became reality almost simultaneously. And Henzler participated in another publication four years later as a scientific advisor. One of the authors was H. B. Strub, Director of the Reichsverband der deutschen landwirtschaftlichen Genossenschaften – Raiffeisen – e.V. He elaborated in detail on how the Führerprinzip had been introduced in the Raiffeisen cooperative and that Anschlusszwang had been a constitutive element in its implementation (see Strub 1938: 66 et seq).

A text by Federation Director Ernst Guenther (the spelling of his surname varies in different versions) was published by the Deutscher Genossenschaftsverlag[41] in 1932, under the rather non-cooperative sounding title "Neue Meister kraft Blut und Arbeit[42]". It is adorned with swastikas in several places and contains the most abhorrent national ideology and extreme racism. Its goal was to contribute to the "rassische Gesundung des deutschen Volkes"[43] (Guenther 1932: 6). The word cooperative, incidentally, does not appear once. The rising demon present in this publication was with all probability still an exception in cooperative federations in

---

41   *German Cooperative Publishing House*
42   *New Master Craftsmen through Blood and Work*
43   *racial purification of the German nation*

1932, but the fact that it was published by the 'Genossenschafts-verlag' clearly indicates that resistance within the cooperative system was already severely weakened.

It should also be noted that the DGV wrote to the Reich Ministry for Economic Affairs in 1936 (the Minister at that time was Hjalmar Schacht) to point out that German cooperatives "had not accepted any Jews as members even before [the National Socialists] took power" (quoted from Fischer 2006: 425).

The Raiffeisen Federation had also instructed its members as early as 1933 to "stop business with Jewish companies and persons. One of the results was that cooperative banks began displaying the signs "Juden unerwünscht"[44] on their counters. (Fischer 2006: 421/422.).

The cooperative federation system 1933 – 1945

Although the clause on Anschlusszwang, introduced by the Act of 1934, applied to all cooperatives equally, it was not applied in equal measures by the DGV. In the period leading up to its introduction, i.e. 1928 to 1933, a total of seven Jewish credit cooperatives were established. They had undergone "auditing by a specifically appointed, independent auditor" After the legislative amendment and facing the threat of dissolution if they were not affiliated to a federation, they tried to save themselves in the only two ways open to them: either by obtaining a right to audit for their own federation or by joining the DGV. These attempts dragged on for quite some time until the responsible authorities, on one hand, refused to grant the federation, now recorded in the association register, the right to audit, and the DGV and its regional federa-

---

44 *Jews unwelcome*

tions, on the other hand, refused to accept Jewish credit cooperatives as members.

The dissolution of the cooperatives concerned was consequently decreed. (See Fischer 2006: 425 et seq).

Let us go back to 1933. At the 69th DGV Congress, Walter Kunze gave a "key speech" "on the status of cooperatives in the National Socialist State", at the end of which he was appointed member of the DGV Board of Directors. He declared, after 30 January 1933, "today we face the great and compelling task of implementing evolution of the entire social, cultural and economic life of our nation. …. It will encompass each individual and the German people as a whole…" In other words: nothing will stay as it is, not even for cooperatives. "As this German evolution is all-encompassing, it also applies to the German cooperative system, to cooperative members themselves and their leaders. The cooperative system cannot lead an independent life but must adapt to our 'Volksleben'[45], taking into account the latter's needs and requirements." Later in this inaugural speech to German commercial cooperatives, he said "It is not greed for profit or selfish aspiration, which has always been at the heart of the cooperative system, but service to the nation and the genuine German common good and preservation of the natural, economic interests of long-established professions. And these are therefore suited to occupying an important role in the National Socialist State." It was on this day at the latest that all the dreams of an independent cooperative life in Germany must have ended. What is tragic is that even after 1945 (and as late as 1995 as we will see later), cooperatives were considered as having remained independent during the National Socialist period. Incidentally, at the end of his speech, Kunze was unanimous-

---

45 *National life*

ly elected as a Board member, raising "rapturous applause". (see Congress of 1933).

To ensure that those who still dreamed of cooperative independence under National Socialism understood where things were going, Gottfried Feder, who was something like the chief economic ideologist of the NSDAP and a party member even before Hitler, also spoke at the Congress. He was State Secretary in the Reich Ministry for Economic Affairs at that time. He proclaimed "Ein Wille ist nunmehr in ganz Deutschland ausschlaggebend, ein Wille befiehlt, und alle Glieder des Deutschen Reiches ordnen sich ihm unter, wissend, daß nur so die Zerrissenheit gebannt, dieses alte grauenhafte deutsche Erbübel des Partikularismus besiegt werden kann."[46] (Congress 1933: 40) So cooperatives and federations too were forced to submit to this one will, if they had not already willingly done so.

Unsurprisingly, the first day of the DGV Congress ended on 25 August 1933 with the following words from Federation Director Schinkel from Hanover "I would not, however, like to end the meeting without asking you to think of our great leader, our Volkskanzler Adolf Hitler and to offer him a triple 'Sieg-Heil!'. (Congress participants rise and join in with the triple 'Sieg-Heil!'.)" (Congress of 1933: 30)

The NSDAP also exercised an extremely rigorous and successful policy with regard to cooperatives and all other social groups. The different cooperative sectors were assigned to different sections of the party. The NSDAP Reichsorganisationsleiter[47] and head of the Deutsche Arbeitsfront (German Labour Front), Robert Ley, took control of consumer cooperatives.

---

46 *"One will is now decisive throughout Germany, one will commands and all members of the German Reich submit to it, knowing that this is the only way to banish inner conflict, to conquer the old, grim, deep-rooted German failing of particularism."*
47 *Leader of the NSDAP party organisation*

Richard Walther Darré, the NSDAP agronomist, became Reich Minister for Agriculture and Reichsbauernführer[48], and therefore took responsibility for the agricultural cooperatives. Adrian von Renteln became President of the DGV. The title of President then also became established in commercial cooperatives – this had already been the case in agricultural cooperatives since the days of Wilhelm Haas.

To mark the anniversary of the National Socialists coming to power, the Bremen and Unterweser district federation of the 'Niedersächsischer Genossenschaftsverband'[49] joined the Edeka Federation in the district of Weser-Ems on 29 January 1934 to organise a "mass gathering of all commercial small and medium-sized businesses". The main speaker was Kunze from the DGV. Over the previous year, he said, Germany had experienced a social revolution. "The accomplishment of this social revolution defined by the Führer is a gigantic task whose completion is not yet in sight and whose practical implementation will demand all our strength and heart. Commercial SME cooperatives also feel called to promote this social revolution." "Throughout his speech, the speaker emphasised that the cooperatives of the last eight decades had to some extent felt like the forerunners of Adolf Hitler's new socialism …" (Bludau 1968: 158/159)

The Reich Minister for Economic Affairs issued a charter for the DGV in October 1936, under which the DGV obtained "full state recognition as the highest auditing and supervisory office" of – commercial - cooperatives (see Bludau 1968: 47). Please note: the state gave the DGV its charter and the federation was the highest supervisory office! This marked an even deeper break from the original principles of cooperatives (and their system). The central federation now officially operated as the controlling

48   *Reich Farmers Leader*
49   *Cooperative Federation for Lower Saxony*

body. Hjalmar Schacht, President of the Reichsbank and Reich Minister for Economic Affairs, spoke at the DGV Congress in 1936 and implemented a radical measure: he appointed Adrian von Renteln President of the DGV. Von Renteln had previously been head of the Hitler Youth Movement, then head of the National Socialist 'Kampfbund für den gewerblichen Mittelstand'[50] and became head of both the 'Reichsstand des deutschen Handels'[51] and the 'Reichsstand des deutschen Handwerks'[52] in May 1933. (see Bracher 1962: 191). Lang, who continued to hold the title of 'Legal Counsellor', saw his responsibility reduced to the auditing system. Three members of the NSDAP were now at the head of the DGV: Kunze, Lang and v. Renteln (see Congress 1936: 9).

The new President held a long inaugural speech in which he also promised "to urge the members of the organisation of which I am in charge to the highest sense of honour, to the highest discipline and the highest economic performance, as only then will it be possible to achieve the difficult tasks we have been set. I realise that it is only with the aid of the National Socialist Führerprinzip that I will be able to tackle these tasks and solve them." He then went on to praise "the exceptional work" of "party members Dr Lang and Dr Kunze". The new President also described the function of the DGV in the economy of Nazi Germany "A truly effective economic leadership" brought the guarantee "that orders issued are also executed". "This close link between the Reich Minister for Economic Affairs and the economy is "safeguarded" by the laws "on the organisational structure of the German economy". The DGV was now also part of this organisation. It "has become the mandatory organisation for commercial cooperatives". Von Renteln then explained in length how the DGV

---

50 *Combat League for the Commercial Middle Class*
51 *Reich Council of German Commerce*
52 *Reich Council of German Trade*

played a role in the economic organisation under the Four Year Plan (see Congress 1936: 21/22). This marked the end of the original German cooperative movement in the commercial sector. What remained was a certain federation system.

I would like to cite a few examples from the abundant evidence available: the first issue of the DGV journal "Blätter für Genossenschaftswesen" for 1941 featured an official message from the DGV Directors: "In the coming year, German commercial cooperatives will once again put all their efforts into supporting the great struggle of the German nation. We also send our warmest greetings to all our cooperative comrades at the front or in special service here at home. We are united behind the motto *"Kampf bis zum Sieg!"*[53] (Blätter für Genossenschaftswesen 1941: 7). This journal had been founded by Schulze!

At the 50th Congress of the Rhine Cooperative in the same year, Federation Director Dr Jongeblodt praised "the victory of our troops on all fronts and associated it with a pledge of allegiance to our Führer". Director v. Lindeiner-Wildau from Berlin "elaborated further on the political tasks of German cooperatives, particularly in the newly recovered areas to the East and West. He pointed out that the outcome of the war would shape the next 1000 years and that even Volksbank Managers had to do everything in their power to bring about an economic contribution to a victorious end." (Blätter für Genossenschaftswesen 1941: 8).

After the German invasion of the Soviet Union on 22 June 1941, Gotthard Ammerlahn wrote an article in the DGV journal entitled "Des Führers Tat – Europas Freiheit"[54]. The following appeared in bold "Moscow believed that it could use the World War unleashed by the Judeo-British plutocrats to then invade

---

53 *Fight until victory*
54 *The Führer's exploits – Europe's Freedom*

a weaker Europe and turn it into wasteland. The Führer once again recognised that the hour was right to put a stop to this new criminal game. The hearts of all Germans, and Germany itself as the heart of Europe, are ablaze in the face of this battle, as they know that a crucial event in world history is currently unfolding: the destruction of the united front of Jewish plutocracy and Bolshevism, the liberation of humanity from a plague that would otherwise be the source of its perish!" (Blätter für Genossenschaftswesen 1941: 201).

Weidmüller, who contributed to legal commentaries on the Cooperative Societies Act both before and after 1945, wrote a commentary on the "Ost-Rechtspflege-Verordnung"[55] of 25 September 1941 and explained amongst other points "§ 5 provides for the possibility of limiting the judicial enforcement of claims by a 'Schutzangehöriger polnischen Volkstums'[56] or a stateless Pole against a German national or an ethnic German, if the court has concerns that the procedure contradicts state or national interests." (Blätter für Genossenschaftswesen 1941: 349) Perhaps he saw things the same way as Globke who only provided a legal commentary on racial laws to prevent the publication of worse comments than his.

Things in the agricultural cooperative federation system did not look any better. The development had been very quick here. Darré, who has already been mentioned earlier, had organised the NSDAP's "agrarpolitischer Apparat"[57] since 1930. Hitler had said to him "Organise the farmers for me, I am giving you a free hand". (See Frank 1988: 75 et seq). Darré was also at the head of the SS Racial Office, later called the

---

55 *Decree of administration of justice in Eastern Territories*
56 *a protected person of Polish tradition*
57 *Instrument for agricultural policy*

Rasse- und Siedlungshauptamt[58]. After 30 January 1933, he worked intensively on taking over all the important management positions in agriculture. All agricultural federations were politically synchronised. Darré became President of the Raiffeisen Federation as early as April 1933. Two months later, he became Reich Minister for Food and Agriculture. He was given the task of "regulating the development of agriculture". This was done by grouping all the previously relevant agricultural organisations into the so-called Reichsnährstand. Darré finally also became Reichbauernführer. "All people or companies involved in agriculture or agricultural products" were then forced to become members of the Reichsnährstand (see Frank 1988: 112 et seq).

Agricultural cooperatives were also included in the Reichsnährstand organisation. They were under the supervision of the "Reichshauptabteilung III"[59], which had the rather odd name "Der Mensch" ('Man'). Agricultural cooperatives – like commercial cooperatives - were "neither affiliated, incorporated nor dissolved. 'A statutory union had (simply) been established between the leadership of the Reichsnährstand and the leadership of the Auditing Federations'. This 'union' was in fact achieved by removing top cooperative managers and placing the Reichbauernführer at the head of the Reichsverband and Landesbauernführer[60] at the head of regional federations." In order to ensure that each individual, smaller cooperative remained obedient, "the Reichsnährstand invented a catalogue of reprisals to force individual cooperatives into line with the Reichsnährstand. A General Meeting had to be held, for example, at the Reichbauernführer's command and the items of the agenda were dictated. The Reichsnährstand's professional tribunals could be used to take action "against 'in-

---

58 *Racial and Settlement Main Office*
59 *Reich Main Department III*
60 *Regional Farmers Leader*

subordinate cooperative board members". They could strip them of their board membership (see Frank 1988: 140 et seq). Bracher speaks of "pseudo-cooperative" institutions in this context in his "Stufen der Machtergreifung" (published nonetheless in 1962) (see Bracher 1962: 180).

The lowest point in the history of cooperatives in Nazi Germany was undoubtedly attained by the following document from the DGV, reproduced by Bludau. It was entitled "Präsident Dr. v. Renteln dankt Generalfeldmarschall Göring."[61] The text read "The commissioner of the Four Year Plan, General Field Marshall Göring, issued a decree on 12 November 1938 for the exclusion of Jews from German economic life, in which § 3 states 'A Jew cannot be a member of a cooperative. Jewish members of cooperatives shall be excluded as at 31 December 1938. No notice of membership termination is necessary.' The great joy with which this decree was received by all German cooperatives was expressed in a telegram of thanks from the President of the DGV to General Field Marshall Göring [...]." (Bludau 1968: 167). A plan by National Socialist leaders (namely Göring, Reich Minister of the Interior Frick, Reich Minister for Economic Affairs Funk, the Head of the Security Police Heydrich) from June 1938 aimed to also appropriate the "business assets of purchasing and trading cooperatives" in the course of the general expropriation of company assets in Jewish hands (see Reich Chancellery files 2008: 447 et seq).

This was the consequence of the "völkische"[62] view on cooperatives, cultivated by the Akademie für Deutsches Recht and supported by Johann Lang, Legal Counsellor of the DGV. Let us have another look at the memorandum issued by the Committee for Cooperative Law at the Akademie für Deutsches Recht

---

61   *President Dr von Renteln thanks General Field Marshall Göring*
62   *nationalist and racist*

which states "The cooperative is rooted in German tradition". It is also sustained by a "commitment to Einordnung[63] and Gemeinschaft"[64]. "It is deeply embedded in German tradition". "… the German character and therefore the German people are intimately acquainted" with the cooperative concept. Cooperatives also had to "demand that every cooperative member be prepared to align himself with the cooperative community and act as a useful component, for the benefit of the nation and the Reich." (Frank 1940: 14 et seq)

Verbandszwang as an expression of the Führerprinzip meant nothing more than a renouncement of the cooperative principles of self-help, self-management, direct responsibility and voluntary action. The cooperatives were part of the totalitarian state and a totally regulated economy, and cooperative organisations played a willing role in the National Socialist power structure. It was no longer possible to speak of a cooperative movement. The cooperative concept had gone to the devil – virtually literally.

The cooperative system and Verbandszwang after 1945

The end of the war in 1945 also – initially - marked the end of central cooperative federations. The specific reasons for this and how these central organisations were then resurrected is not of central importance here. But it is rather strange to see how the official and semi-official historiography of the cooperative system glosses over the year 1945 with a few feeble words. A history of the central federation for commercial cooperatives, which was

---

63   *alignment*
64   *community*

resurrected under the former name of 'Deutscher Genossenschaftsverband' (DGV) in 1948, appeared in 1972, i.e. not too long afterwards. It, however, only includes the brief statement "The work of the Deutscher Genossenschaftsverband ended with the collapse of the German Reich. Attempts by legal counsellor Dr Lang to re-establish the federation from Berlin failed". It was then finally resurrected in 1948 as a result of the gradual expansion of the labour communities belonging to the still existing regional auditing federations. (Lukas 1972: 35).

Even the book 'Geschichte des deutschen Genossenschaftswesen'[65] by Helmut Faust (the only relatively comprehensive history available), whose third edition appeared in 1977, i.e. also quite close afterwards, has little to say on the period concerning the end of the war. Faust in fact does not write a single word about the fate of the DGV in 1945, only stating that the end of the war brought about "virtual chaos" (Faust 1977: 310). With regard to the central agricultural federation, he does however add "The political and economic collapse of the German Reich in 1945 signalled the end of central cooperative federations", the Raiffeisen Federation "had to be liquidated" (Faust 1977: 430/431). I shall overlook the fact that nothing collapsed in 1945 (other than the views and ideology of devout National Socialists); Germany did however suffer a total military and political defeat.

In another semi-official history of the cooperative system by Aschhoff und Henningsen, published by the Deutsche Genossenschaftsbank[66] in 1995, only the following lines are written with regard to 1945: "All central organisations ceased to exist at the end of the war or had to be dissolved." (Aschhoff/Henningsen 1995: 38/39).

---

65 *History of the German Cooperative System*
66 *German Cooperative Bank*

Whatever happened to the German cooperative system in 1945, the familiar federation structures were largely re-established by the end of the 1940s. However, how were the years before 1945 viewed in these structures? A series of statements are available from 1951. In this year, Lang and Weidmüller once again published their legal commentary on the Cooperative Societies Act, as leading federation representatives and legal experts of the DGV, for the first time since 1945. It was carefully cleansed of all praise of National Socialism but lacked, however, any criticism of relevant legislation on cooperatives from the National Socialist period. On the contrary, the text on article 54 remained unaltered – and still had the heading "Anschlußzwang" (see Lang/ Weidmüller 1951). There was not yet any mention of 'Pflichtmitgliedschaft' (compulsory membership).

Letschert also published a new edition of his book on cooperative auditing in 1951. Regarding the introduction of Verbandszwang, he wrote "Even though only a small portion of cooperatives were not affiliated to federations before 1934, there were few complaints from cooperative circles following the introduction of Verbandszwang, which is the best proof that the cooperatives saw this obligation as necessary and useful, and still see it as so today." (Letschert 1951: 26). This declaration still embodies the essence of the 1930s in Germany and entirely negates the spirit with which cooperatives were once established. If one follows Letschert, the concept of freedom, of direct responsibility had been perverted to such an extent that forced obligation was viewed as necessary and useful. Letschert, however, demonstrates enormous cynicism when claiming that an absence of complaints on the issue of forced obligation provided proof of consent at a time of National Socialist terror. He does nonetheless admit (without seeming to be aware of the blatant contradiction with cooperative principles) that "The amendment of 1934 considerably restricted the freedom of cooperatives." (Letschert 1951: 27).

In the 4th issue of the magazine 'Zeitschrift für das gesamte Genossenschaftswesen' of 1951, the year of its creation, a few articles refer to the period between 1933 and 1945. Henzler, who we are familiar with from 1934, for example, wrote about the "legitimacy of Anschlußzwang which had been requested by all branches of German cooperatives and was firmly anchored in the German Cooperative Societies Act." (Henzler 1951: 204). In view of Henzler's close proximity to the implementation of Anschlusszwang, this false statement can indeed be considered as more than just mere forgetfulness. It can confidently be described as a lie.

Johannes Lang also minimised the importance of the amendment to the Cooperative Societies Act of 1934 when he seemingly innocently declared "Anschlusszwang is merely a necessity based on lessons learnt from the past. …Once cooperatives are obliged to be audited by an auditing federation with the right to audit, in the same way as joint stock companies are audited by publically-appointed auditors, the obligation to be affiliated to an auditing federation for this purpose is not to be viewed as a forced confederacy but only as a logical measure to ensure the implementation of statutory compulsory auditing." (Lang 1951: 256). However, Lang then proceeded to land the cooperative system with an unpleasant surprise with his next sentence, in which he wrote "In a controlled economy, the state cannot renounce such means of influencing the economy" (ibid.). Lang had obviously still not noticed in 1951 that the time of state control and a controlled economy, as operated under National Socialism and on which he and Ludwig Weidmüller had approvingly commented, had been ended by the politician Ludwig Erhards back in 1948/49 at the latest, and that the country had now adopted a market economy. If Lang is to be taken seriously, the state should therefore be able to forego Anschlusszwang and other such similar measures in a market economy.

Lang had no qualms at describing the memorandum issued by the Akademie für Deutsches Recht in 1940, which was to provide the foundation for a "völkisches law" even in the sector of cooperatives, as a model. "Suggestions for editorial changes to the Cooperative Societies Act and legal and technical changes were dealt with thoroughly in the memorandum by the Committee for Cooperative Law of that time and I therefore refer to the recommendations made in this document." (Lang 1951: 257). Although he is certainly referring to formal and technical provisions, he does however overlook the fact that the Cooperative Societies Act clearly reflected "National Socialist ideology" by 1940, as he himself had commented two years earlier, and that the work by the Akademie für Deutsches Recht formed the foundation for its advanced development "in line with National Socialist principles". (Lang/Weidmüller 1938: 12).

Two other authors also recommended that the work by the Akademie für Deutsches Recht on cooperative law should not be allowed to fall into oblivion – this also appeared in the 4th issue of the 'Zeitschrift für das gesamte Genossenschaftswesen' in 1951. Both authors, like Johannes Lang, had belonged to its Committee on Cooperatives. They were Reinhold Henzler (see Henzler 1951: 187) and Georg Schröder, who referred to the fact that the text on the Cooperative Societies Act was "ready to be adopted" and said that "the text survived the war and could today form the foundation for a continuation of this work". (Schröder 1951: 225)

The last article from this issue of the 'Zeitschrift für das gesamte Genossenschaftswesen' which is worth mentioning in this context was written by a cooperative research scientist, Heinz Paulick. It begins with a semantic whitewash, using the term "Pflichtmitgliedschaft" – for what seems to be the very first time

- (Paulick 1951: e. g. 266), although it does still mention "Anschlußzwang" (Paulick 1951: e. g. 265). Paulick also evokes the myth – if not to say lie – of the cooperatives' desire for Anschlusszwang, which presumably prevailed from that time onwards. He was very clear on this "The reasons for which the legislator revoked the freedom of cooperatives to decide whether or not they wanted to join an auditing federation, in favour of compulsory membership, can be found in the repeated requests from cooperatives for such a provision. Ausschlußzwang [!] was not forced on cooperatives by the legislator unilaterally against their will, but was introduced and systematically expanded at the instigation of the cooperatives themselves, and not the cooperative federations." (Paulick 1951: 267; my emphasis). Paulick did not hesitate to attribute Anschlusszwang to the prompting of cooperatives, and not that of cooperative federations. Which cooperatives were then meant to have been involved here, those that were already federation members – if so why? – or those who were not affiliated? It would have been easier for the latter to achieve this by simply joining a federation.

When the question of cooperative law was discussed in the Federal Republic of Germany in both political and economic circles at the start of the 1950s, the Bundestag[67] and Bundesrat[68] petitioned the Federal Government in 1954 to "check the current law on cooperatives and to quickly begin preliminary work on a reform". The Federal Minister for Justice subsequently appointed a commission of experts to clarify fundamental matters (see Neumayer 1956: 3).

The material and reports drawn up by this commission were then published by the Federal Ministry for Justice in three volumes between 1956 and 1959. The unavoidable Johann Lang was

---

67   *Federal Parliament*
68   *Federal Council*

also a member of this commission. He, however, left the topic of Verbandszwang, which was now almost unanimously referred to as Pflichtmitgliedschaft to others. It was therefore Ernst von Caemmerer, who had been a law professor in Freiburg/Breisgau for decades, who dealt with this issue. In doing so, he elaborated on the story that the statutory provision of 1934 was "the result of lessons learnt from the previous economic crisis" (see Caemmerer 1959: 10/11). He describes everything that "the" legislator had intended with this law in 1934, but there is not one single sentence on the fact that "the" legislator in Germany at that time had been Hitler's Reich Government alone since the Enabling Act of 23 March 1933 (see Caemmerer 1959: 30/31). According to Caemmerer, the "reform" of 1934 was "not (the product) of National Socialist ideology. It was instead based on the conclusions of cooperative experience, which accepted the necessity of restricting cooperative self-management for the purpose of implementing an effective audit inspection, in the interests of a healthy cooperative system." (Caemmerer 1959: 31) It was obviously a matter of healthy cooperatives in a healthy state in 1934. In reality, however, as we have already seen, 'the cooperative system' was as diseased as the state system itself.

Nevertheless, the DGRV[69] opted not to belong to the worldwide cooperative organisation, the International Cooperative Alliance (ICA), during the Cold War years as the ICA also admitted cooperatives from the communist bloc. Their heavy dependence on the party and the state contradicted the principles of free and independent cooperatives in the eyes of the DGRV. This view may be perfectly acceptable – it should also, however, have been applied to its own past under the National Socialist state.

---

69   *Deutscher Genossenschafts- und Raiffeisenverband*

The commemorative publication issued by the Deutscher Genossenschaftsverband to mark its centenary in 1959 also needs
a mention. This describes such important events as the affiliation of the 'Verband der Eisenbahn-Spar- und Darlehnskassen'[70],
founded in 1906, to the DGV in 1938. It would be interesting to
know whether this affiliation was voluntary or forced on it by the
legislation of 1934, according to which each auditing federation
had to belong to a central federation. It then says "The commercial cooperative system therefore achieved the cohesion, which
still exists today, within the Deutscher Genossenschaftsverband
as the central federation." It is astounding to see how National
Socialism left the cooperative system with such a positive legacy.
The following statement is extremely ambiguous: "The cooperative system had to pool and deploy all its ideological strength
again after 1933 as National Socialism did not initially want
to concede any room for cooperatives in its economic system."
DGV 1959: 697). The cooperative system therefore obviously had
to align itself intensively with National Socialist ideology so that
it no longer appeared as a hindrance to National Socialism. And
then there is this embarrassing untruth: "Dr Lang successful-
ly resisted the introduction of the Führerprinzip in cooperatives, which signified nothing more than the relinquishment of
self-help and direct responsibility, both orally and in writing as
well as in the Committee for Cooperatives at the Akademie für
Deutsches Recht." (see DGV 1959: 69/70)

I also consulted Helmut Faust, the author of the only comprehensive history of cooperatives, whom I quoted earlier. His
"Geschichte der Genossenschaftsbewegung"[71] was first published in 1958 and its third and last edition appeared in 1977
and has semi-official credentials in view of Faust's earlier ac-

---

70   *Federation of Railway, Savings and Loan Cooperatives*
71   *History of the Cooperative Movement*

tivities in the cooperative sector. He says that of the two Legal Counsellors at the head of the DGV in 1933, one was Johann Lang, "an exceptionally competent, experienced legal expert" – the other, Karl Korthaus, on the other hand adhered "unconditionally to the National Socialist Movement". He saw "the radical political changes of 1933" as "a turning point in the fate of the German nation". Korthaus had in fact written in the DGV journal that it would be "a disaster if the cooperative representatives were now to stand sulkily to one side and not take the pulse of the time". For Faust, this was an expression of "pure idealism". In the sentence that followed, Faust (again) let slip an incredible minimisation of National Socialist policy "the brave man was spared from having to witness how soon the National Socialist usurpers in Germany ignored the constitution, set up a political dictatorship, destroyed freedom, flouted law and finally led the country into the catastrophe of the Second World War…" (Faust 1977: 307/308). Korthaus indeed died on 15 December 1933 - he therefore did actually have time to experience everything which Faust believed he had been spared (except the war): the establishment of a political dictatorship, the destruction of freedom, the flouting of law and much more. Faust too had lived through the year 1933. However, the destruction of a democratic, constitutional Republic and daily acts of brutality merely represented a "radical political change" in his eyes.

Faust displays admirable moderation when writing of Johann Lang, "In the years between 1933 and 1945, the main goal was to ensure that the cooperative principles of self-management and direct responsibility did not completely wither away in the face of the administrative Führerprinzip enforced by the oppressive National Socialist regime, which was certainly no easy task." (Faust 1977: 310).

Faust is more honest when it comes to the agricultural cooperatives. Faust presents the appropriate passages on the "Reichsverband der deutschen landwirtschaftlichen Genossenschaften – Raiffeisen – e.V." under the heading "Downfall of 1933 – 1945". He remarks that the agricultural sector had flirted with National Socialism even before 1933, that there had been cooperative leaders "who had adopted National Socialist ideology as their own and had attempted to disseminate it within the cooperatives". The "entire agricultural organisation" had been "politically infiltrated by the NSDAP's well-organised agrarpolitischen Apparat". "The National Socialist's takeover in 1933 then however hit even agricultural cooperatives like a raging torrent. The National Socialists conquered any resistance with 'brute force'. It resulted in a complete restructuring of the organisation." (Faust 1977: 425/426)

With regard to the relationship between consumer cooperatives and National Socialism, Faust correctly observes "Both movements defended principles which were incompatible. Totalitarian dictatorship on one hand, democratic organisation on the other. The National Socialists used unchecked propaganda to win over the middle classes, primarily retailers, who had always viewed consumer cooperatives as fierce rivals. The National Socialists' demagogic slogans found fertile soil in these stratums of society." Faust then goes on to describe in relative detail how the ruling powers absorbed and destroyed consumer cooperatives (see Faust 1977: 485 et seq).

Finally, reference should also be made to the revised publication by Gunter Aschhoff und Eckart Henningsen of 1995 in this context – the cooperative system's view of the Nazi period. It was published by the DG-Verlag (German Cooperative Publishing House) and is therefore attributed a semi-official quality.

The authors group factual developments spanning several eras under one heading: "The period between 1918 and 1945". This sounds as though there had been no significant turning point during the course of these 28 years, and that it only occurred in 1945. However, the first sentence under this heading does separate the period into two time spans: "The period from the end of World War I to the end of World War II is subdivided into the years up to 1933, and the subsequent period of controlled economy with the war from 1939 to 1945." So nothing else happened in 1933 other than the introduction of a controlled economy. The year 1934 does however also earn a mention in other respects: "The cooperative organisation was given special status in 1934 when a legislative amendment enhanced the existing compulsory auditing of cooperatives dating back to 1889 with compulsory membership of an auditing federation ..." This is a remarkable misinterpretation – regardless of the National Socialist background to Anschlusszwang: forced obligation to join an organisation was therefore nothing more than the enhancement of an auditing obligation. It later reads "Increasing integration in the controlled economy ... affected cooperatives differently. Cooperatives established on the basis of democratic self-management had no place in the socio-political and economic concept of National Socialism on principle, but had been able to acquire such a strong position in the market that they could simply not be dissolved." (Aschhoff/Henningsen 1995: 33 et seq)

Do the authors really believe that the cooperatives had been as strong as only the Church, which could also not simply be dissolved? Were they really stronger than all political parties, than trade unions which were all dissolved? Were the cooperatives stronger than German Regional States whose autonomy had been entirely abolished? Do the authors wish to claim that they had never heard of the National Socialist policy of Gleichschaltung? A glance at one of the numerous works published on National Socialist rule since the middle of the 1950s, in particular that of Karl

Dietrich Bracher (see e. g. Bracher 1962: 186 et seq and Bracher 1993: 238/239) would undoubtedly have enlightened Aschhoff and Henningsen on how the strongest opponents of National Socialism were so demolished that mere empty shells remained at the best.

The authors nonetheless knew that things happened differently in "only" one single sector, that of consumer cooperatives. "Its socialist activities were prohibited by the destruction of its supporting organisations", (see Aschhoff/Henningsen 1995: 37). This is a shocking choice of wording which also demonstrates extreme ignorance. Anyone writing about "The German Cooperative System" under the auspices of the Deutsche Genossenschaftsbank, should actually know that the supporting organisations of cooperatives, including consumer cooperatives, were none other than their members. It was the consumer cooperative organisations, including the federation allied to the catholic movement, which were destroyed after 1933. And the latter was not very inclined to undertake "socialist activities" by its very nature and tradition. It is alarming to see that the authors are naïve enough to readily adopt the National Socialist justification for the destruction of consumer cooperatives by using the term "sozialistisch orientierte Aktivitäten"[72]. "The NSDAP's battle against consumer cooperatives as an undesirable form of large-scale retail in Germany" had in fact already taken place before 1933 – as can be read under the appropriate chapter heading in Kurzer's "Nationalsozialismus und Konsumgenossenschaften" (see Kurzer 1997: 56 et seq.).

According to our two authors, federations of rural cooperatives "essentially" retained "the autonomy of their auditing functions – extended by the cooperative legislative amendment of

---

1934 – and their other supervisory functions." We are now aware of how absurd this statement is. (See Aschhoff/Henningsen 1995: 37/38)

It is noticeable that Austria has a much more accurate view of the period of National Socialist rule which began with the Anschluss[73] , the annexation of Austria by Germany in 1938. A history of Austrian cooperatives which appeared in 1997 clearly observes that after the Anschluss in 1938,"the Austrian federation of cooperatives very quickly felt the effects of the trait which characterised the oppressive National Socialist regime: force". "Total Gleichschaltung" occurred. And the years 1938 to 1945 were "not to be seen as true cooperative history" as "essential requirements of a pure cooperative system were lacking". (Brazda/Schediwy/Todev 1997: 210 et seq). The German cooperative system in contrast has supressed everything, until today.

Cosmetic changes to terminology – the replacement of the word Verbandszwang by Pflichtmitgliedschaft – by federations are, incidentally, almost understandable. Pflicht means duty or obligation which has a moral connotation. Zwang, on the other hand, implies force or coercion which only sounds ugly and unpleasant. The fact, however, that legal scholars adopt such self-serving declarations, which can easily be proved to be incorrect, leaves readers uneasy. What can be thought of such comments in the face of such scientific dishonesty? At least the author of the entry "Cooperative history" in the Handwörterbuch des Genossenschaftswesens[74], published in 1980, Hugo Tillmann, still calls it by its official name: 'Anschlusszwang' (see Tillmann 1980: 783).

---

73   *Annexation of Austria by Germany*
74   *Concise Dictionary of the Cooperative System*

No Anschlusszwang – more cooperative freedom

It is curious how the quasi-official cooperative system is automatically on the defensive when facing any opposition to Anschlusszwang. The 'Zeitschrift für das gesamte Genossenschaftswesen' printed an article by Fabian Wolfgang Heß entitled "Die Pflichtmitgliedschaft in den Prüfungsverbänden auf dem Prüfstand"[75] in the 4th issue of 2009. The title already betrays Heß's critical view of this issue. He is clear enough when he says "The constantly reiterated argument of safeguarding cooperatives from insolvency is particularly unconvincing. There is no question of the fact that cooperative insolvency is rare. However, whether this can be exclusively attributed to compulsory membership in federations is more than questionable." Moreover, there are other instruments available to avoid threatening insolvency, for example the protection schemes offered by the National Association of German Cooperative Banks (BVR) for banks or the additional option of fusions. Minimum capital requirements are another possibility, as "if sufficient capital is available to guarantee the necessary protection of creditors, the motive behind compulsory membership disappears, meaning that compulsory auditing by federations is no longer necessary." And "there are no reservations with regard to a free choice of auditor from a professional point of view, at least not since the qualification requirements for auditors were raised by the last amendments to the WPO" (Heß 2009: 290/291; WPO means Code of Professional Practice for German Public Auditors). Now the fact that the magazine, which does have some weight in the cooperative system, published this critical observation should have earned

---

75 *Compulsory membership of auditing federations under close scrutiny*

it some recognition, were it not firstly obvious that an academic magazine should also publish critical articles and secondly if it had not added the following annotation "The views expressed are the author's own" (Heß 2009: 285). Who else's should they be? Are all other articles blessed with the consensual approval of the 'Weltgeist'[76]? Or are they only published with the express approval of the President of the Deutscher Genossenschafts- und Raiffeisenverband? A curious episode, which raises the question of how dependent or independent cooperative science actually is of cooperative federations.

Back to the facts: it is indisputable that cooperative insolvency is very rare. Official statistics show, for example, that 1.58% of private companies and corporate enterprises in Germany became insolvent in 2009, in contrast to only 0.24% of cooperatives (see Kaltenborn 2014: 181). These are extremely satisfactory figures for members of cooperatives. It is, however, inexplicable why the DGRV chooses to give a rather unreliable presentation of the facts. In its business report for 2013, it reports that GmbHs[77] were affected by 41.9% of all insolvency proceedings in 2012, and that only 0.1% concerned cooperatives (see DGRV 2013: 7). This, however, means nothing if I do not know what percentage of companies these legal forms represent. What is actually interesting is to see how the percentage of insolvency proceedings differs in relation to the percentage of companies.

Anschlusszwang is unique to Germany. German cooperative legislation and its practice also involve so-called 'Gründungsprüfungen'[78]. Here the auditing federation issues a certificate confirming that the new cooperative has been admitted as a member of the federation. An "expert statement from the auditing feder-

---

76   *"World spirit"*

77   *German form of a limited company*

78   *Initial audits*

ation" is then required on whether "the interests of cooperative members or creditors are at risk given the personal or economic conditions, particularly the cooperative's net asset position" – as stipulated by § 11, para. 2, no. 3 of the Cooperative Societies Act. In the federations' view, this Gründungsprüfung is also a key factor in ensuring that the insolvency rate is so low.

Doubts can, however, also be raised regarding this statement. 2012 saw the publication of an "Opinion of the European Economic and Social Committee" (EESC) of the EU on "cooperatives and restructuring". It reaches the following general conclusion: "in times of crisis cooperatives are more resilient and stable than other forms of enterprise" (EESC 2012: 2 and 7). In Sweden, for example, "the mortality rate of cooperatives is lower than for conventional enterprises" (EESC 2012: 10) and in the UK, the number of cooperatives has increased by 10% since 2009, whilst the overall number of companies fell by 4.9%. (EESC 2012: 9). In its summary, the opinion of the EESC attributes this to the "specificity of the cooperative enterprises", namely "their long-term approach, their strong territorial roots, their promotion of members' interests, and their focus on cooperation among themselves" (EWSA 2012: 1).

While we are looking abroad, let us note that Italy has neither Gründungsprüfungen nor Anschlusszwang. However, still only 0.2% of cooperatives became insolvent in Italy in 2009, the same percentage as in Germany. Insolvency, however, concerned 0.6% of other forms of enterprise. "One look at insolvency statistics is enough to understand the difference in stability between cooperatives and other types of company". (Seifert 2013: 29). In Italy, cooperatives last longer than other corporate legal forms. Of the companies in existence in 2003, 41.4% of cooperatives had been established before 1990; this figure was only 26.3% for other forms of enterprise (Seifert 2013: 26). This confirms Heß's aforementioned theory that there are other reasons behind the financial resilience of cooperatives than Anschlusszwang and auditing by a federation. Seifert lists them in more detail in relation to Italy, citing, above all, the major importance of diverse incentives fixed by law, making it easier to constitute and safeguard capital reserves. Seifert also describes the cooperative economy as much more sustainable. (See Seifert 2013: 33 et seq and 50/51).

Furthermore, there is reason enough to ask ourselves another question. Why shouldn't cooperatives have to fulfil the same requirements as any other company? The German economic system is based on the principles of a market economy. This involves responsibility and autonomy, and willingness to bear the risks which are intrinsic to market developments. A federation such as the DGRV loses its credibility if it advocates a market economy on one hand but wants to protect its members from its dangers on the other. Members of cooperatives are not less intelligent, less qualified or weaker in character than others who venture to engage in economic activities. Why then should they be protected from the rigours of the market by a glass dome? It may be true that the "cooperative" entity itself deserves more protection than other market players, as bad decisions by the Executive Board, which acts independently despite the participation rights of its members, can unexpectedly damage them – the members. To prevent this, the audit requirements for cooperatives could and should be slightly stricter than for other corporate legal forms. That should, however, be enough.

A second point is also worth mentioning: a cooperative federation recently got into serious economic difficulties and had to cease its activities. This was the Mitteldeutscher Genossenschaftsverband (MGV), which was only saved from the threat of insolvency proceedings by fusion with the 'Genossenschaftsverband e.V.' (which absorbed it), in 2013 (see Kaltenborn 2014: 297

et seq.). This cancels out the cooperative federation system's own argument that only federation membership could protect cooperatives from insolvency. The German cooperative system must now indeed be prepared to accept the fact that even a federation, whose expertise is intended to help cooperatives survive, is not immune from financial ruin as a result of economic incompetence. This was actually inconceivable, but it has happened and there is no guarantee that it will not happen again. It would now be ridiculous for cooperative federations to maintain that compulsory membership offers a safe haven for all cooperatives.

In short, it is now high time to undo the legislative amendment of 1934. This does not have to be in full but enforced membership should at last be revoked, as is already the case in Austria. The situation across the border indeed offers an opportunity for prior analysis of the consequences of such a revocation. 2014 saw the 80th anniversary of the disastrous amendment of 1934. It would not be a bad idea to restore something of the Schulze tradition after eight decades. His goal had ultimately been to create *free* cooperatives in a free society.

Bibliography

ADR Vol. I 1986 Werner Schubert, Werner Schmidt and Jürgen Regge (eds.): Akademie für Deutsches Recht 1933 – 1945. Protokolle der Ausschüsse. Vol. I Ausschuss für Aktienrecht, Werner Schubert. Berlin-New York.

ADR Vol. IV 1989 Werner Schubert, Werner Schmidt and Jürgen Regge (eds.): Akademie für Deutsches Recht 1933 – 1945. Protokolle der Ausschüsse. Vol. IV Ausschuss für Genossenschaftsrecht, Werner Schubert. Berlin-New York.

Aschhoff/Henningsen 1995 Gunter Aschhoff and Eckart Henningsen: Das deutsche Genossenschaftswesen. Entwicklung, Struktur, wirtschaftliches Potential. (Publications of DG Bank Deutsche Genossenschaftsbank, Vol. 15). 2nd revised and extended edition Frankfurt am Main.

Bernhardt 1889 Bernhardt : Folgen des neuen Genossenschaftsgesetzes. In: Blätter für Genossenschaftswesen. (Innung der Zukunft XXXVI. Jg.) Publ. of Allgemeiner Verband deutscher Erwerbs- und Wirthschaftsgenossenschaften.

Beuthien 2011 Volker Beuthien: Genossenschaftsgesetz mit Umwandlungs- und Kartellrecht sowie Statut der Europäischen Gemeinschaft, co-editors Reinmar Wolff and Martin Schöpflin (Beck'sche Kurz-Kommentare Vol. 11). 15th, revised and extended ed. Munich.

Blätter für Genossenschaftswesen 1941 88. Jg.

Bludau 1968 Kuno Bludau: Nationalsozialismus und Genossenschaften. Hannover.

Bracher 1962 Karl Dietrich Bracher: Stufen der Machtergreifung. In: Karl Dietrich Bracher, Wolfgang Sauer and Gerhard Schulz: Die nationalsozialistische Machtergreifung. Studien zur Errichtung des totalitären Herrschaftssystems in Deutschland 1933/34. 2nd, revised ed. Cologne and Opladen.

Bracher 1993 Karl Dietrich Bracher: Die deutsche Diktatur. Entstehung Struktur Folgen des Nationalsozialismus. 7th ed. Cologne.

Brazda/Schediwy/Todev 1997 Johann Brazda, Robert Schediwy and Tode Todev: Selbsthilfe oder politisierte Wirtschaft. Zur Geschichte des Österreichischen Genossenschaftsverbandes (Schulze-Delitzsch) 1872 – 1997. Vienna.

Caemmerer 1959 Ernst von Caemmerer: Pflichtmitgliedschaft bei Prüfungsverbänden; Rechtsbehelfe gegen die Verweigerung der Aufnahme in einen Prüfungsverband. In: Federal Ministry for Justice (ed.): Zur Reform des Genossenschaftsrechts. Referate und Materialien. Vol. 3 Bonn.

DGRV 2013 DGRV – Deutscher Genossenschafts- und Raiffeisenverband e.V. (ed.): Business report 2012. DGRV. The Cooperatives. Berlin.

DGV 1959 Deutscher Genossenschaftsverband (Schulze-Delitzsch) e.V. (ed.): Commemorative publication on the centenary of Deutscher Genossenschaftsverband (Schulze-Delitzsch) e.V. Bonn.

EESC 2012 European Economic and Social Committee: "Opinion of the European Economic and Social Committee on "cooperatives and restructuring" (own-initiative opinion). CCMI/093 „Cooperatives and restructuring". Brüssels.

Faust 1967 Helmut Faust: Die Zentralbank der deutschen Genossenschaften. Vorgeschichte, Aufbau, Aufgaben und Entwicklung der Deutschen Genossenschaftskasse.

Faust 1977 Helmut Faust: Geschichte der Genossenschaftsbewegung. Ursprung und Aufbruch der Genossenschaftsbewegung in England, Frankreich und Deutschland sowie ihre weitere Entwicklung im deutschen Sprachraum. 3rd, revised and extended ed. Frankfurt/Main.

Feldmann 1936 Walter Feldmann: Die Rechtsstellung des Prüfers (Revisors) und der Prüfungsverbände (Revisionsverbände) bei den Erwerbs- und Wirtschaftsgenossenschaften in ihrer Entwicklung und nach geltendem Recht (Unter Berücksichtigung des Wirtschaftsprüferrechts und der Pflichtprüfung im Aktienrecht). Inaugural-Dissertation an der Rechts- und Staatswissenschaftlichen Fakultät der Universität zu Freiburg im Breisgau. Freiburg.

Fischer 2006 Albert Fischer: Jüdische Genossenschaftsbanken im nationalsozialistischen Deutschland 1933 – 1938. In: Vierteljahreshefte für Zeitgeschichte. 54th set. Issue 3.

Frank 1988 Claudia Frank: Der „Reichsnährstand" und seine Ursprünge. Struktur, Funktion und ideologische Konzeption. Hamburg.

Frank 1940 Hans Frank (Hrsg.): Das Recht der deutschen Genossenschaften. Memorandum. Committee for Cooperative Law at the Akademie für Deutsches Recht (ed.). Walter Granzow (Working reports of Akademie für Deutsches Recht published by its President Reichsminister Hans Frank. Tübingen.

Cooperative Societies Act (GenG) 1867. Gesetz, betreffend die privatrechtliche Stellung der Erwerbs- und Wirthschaftsgenossenschaften. 27 March 1867. Gesetzessammlung für die Königlichen Preußischen Staaten 1867 no. 34.

Cooperative Societies Act (GenG) 1871. Gesetz, betreffend die Deklaration des Gesetzes vom 4. Juli 1868. 19 May 1871. Reichs-Gesetzblatt 1871 no. 21.

Cooperative Societies Act (GenG) 1889. Gesetz, betreffend die Erwerbs- und Wirthschaftsgenossenschaften. 1 May 1889. In: Reichs-Gesetzblatt. 1889. No. 11

Coperative Societies Act (GenG) 1934. Gesetz zur Änderung des Genossenschaftsgesetzes. 30 October 1934. Reichsgesetzblatt I 1934. No. 122.

Cooperative Societies Act (GenG) Substantiation 1934. Begründung zum Gesetz zur Aenderung des Genossenschaftsgesetzes. 30 October 1934 (RGBl. I No. 122). In: Reichsanzeiger und Preußischer Staatsanzeiger, 1934 No. 256, Berlin, Thursday, 1 November 1934, evening.

Genossenschaftstag 1930. 67th Congress of Deutscher Genossenschaftsverband e.V. in Hamburg from 31 August to 3 September 1930. Berlin.

Genossenschaftstag 1932. 68th Congress of Deutscher Genossenschaftsverband e.V. in Hamburg. 21 to 24 August 1932. Berlin.

Genossenschaftstag 1933. 69th Congress of Deutscher Genossenschaftsverband e.V. in Hamburg. 25 to 26 August 1933. Berlin.

Genossenschaftstag 1936 Report on the 71st Congress of Deutscher Genossenschaftsverband. 11 December 1936. Berlin.

Glenk 1996 Hartmut Glenk: Die eingetragene Genossenschaft. Munich.

Glenk 2013 Hartmut Glenk: Genossenschaftsrecht. Systematik und Praxis des Genossenschaftswesens. 2nd, revised ed. Munich.

Guenther 1932 Ernst Guenther: Neue Meister kraft Blut und Arbeit. Versuch zur Neuordnung und zum Schutz des Deutschen Handwerks, Deutschen Handels und Deutschen Gewerbes. Berlin.

Henzler 1934 Reinhold Henzler: Erneuerung des deutschen Genossenschaftswesens. Berlin.

Henzler 1951 Reinhold Henzler: Das Genossenschaftsgesetz – ein Mittel zur Erhaltung der genossenschaftlichen Eigenart. In: Zeitschrift für das gesamt Genossenschaftswesen. Vol. I 1951, Issue 3/4.

Henzler 1970 Reinhold Henzler: Der genossenschaftliche Grundauftrag: Förderung der Mitglieder. Gesammelte Abhandlungen und Beiträge. Frankfurt/Main.

Heß 2009 Fabian Wolfgang Heß: Die Pflichtmitgliedschaft in den Prüfungsverbänden auf dem Prüfstand. In: Zeitschrift für das gesamte Genossenschaftswesen. Vol. 59, Issue 4/2009.

Kaltenborn 2012a Wilhelm Kaltenborn: Ein großes deutsches Leben. In: Wilhelm Kaltenborn: Vision und Wirklichkeit. Beiträge zur Idee und Geschichte von Genossenschaften. Berlin.

Kaltenborn 2012b Wilhelm Kaltenborn: Schulze-Delitzsch und die soziale Frage. In: Wilhelm Kaltenborn: Vision und Wirklichkeit. Beiträge zur Idee und Geschichte von Genossenschaften. Berlin.

Kaltenborn 2014 Wilhelm Kaltenborn: Schein und Wirklichkeit. Genossenschaften und Genossenschaftsverbände. Eine kritische Auseinandersetzung. Berlin.

Kaufmann 1903 Heinrich Kaufmann (Hrsg.): Jahrbuch des Zentralverbandes deutscher Konsumvereine. First ed. 1903. Hamburg.

Kurzer 1997 Ulrich Kurzer: Nationalsozialismus und Konsumgenossenschaften. Gleichschaltung, Sanierung und Teilliquidation zwischen 1933 und 1935. Pfaffenweiler.

Lang 1951 Johann Lang: Anregungen, Wünsche und Forderungen zur Reform des deutschen Genossenschaftsrechts. b) Vom

Standpunkt der gewerblichen Genossenschaften. In: Zeitschrift für das gesamte Genossenschaftswesen. Vol. I 1951 Issue 3/4.

Lang/Weidmüller 1938 Johannes Lang und Ludwig Weidmüller: Das Reichsgesetz, betreffend die Erwerbs- und Wirtschaftgenossenschaften. Kleiner Kommentar von Ludolf Parisius und Hans Crüger. 23rd revised and extended ed. Berlin.

Lang/Weidmüller 1951 Johannes Lang und Ludwig Weidmüller, Gesetz, betreffend die Erwerbs- und Wirtschaftsgenossenschaften. Kleiner Kommentar. 26th, revised and extended ed. of the text version of Parisius and Crüger. Berlin.

Lang/Weidmüller 2011 Genossenschaftsgesetz (Gesetz betreffend die Erwerbs- und Wirtschaftsgenossenschaften). Mit Erläuterungen zum Umwandlungsgesetz. Kommentar, bearbeitet von Hans-Jürgen Schaffland u. a. Mit Erläuterungen zum Recht der Wohnungsgenossenschaften von Uwe Hannis/g. 37th, revised ed. Berlin/Boston.

Letschert 1921 Reinhold Letschert: Die Durchführung der Verbandsrevision im Deutschen Genossenschaftsverband. 2nd, completely revised and extended ed. Berlin.

Letschert 1927 Reinhold Letschert: Die Revision der Genossenschaft. Ein Leitfaden für die Praxis. 3rd, completely revised and extended ed. Berlin.

Letschert 1951 Reinhold Letschert: Die genossenschaftliche Pflichtprüfung. 5th, completely revised and extended ed. Wiesbaden-Biedrich.

Lukas 1972 Klaus Lukas: Der Deutsche Genossenschaftsverband. Entwicklung, Struktur und Funktion. Berlin.

Michalski 2010 Lutz Michalski: Syst. Darstellung 1: Überblick über das GmbH-Recht. In: Lutz Michalski (Hrsg.): Kommentar zum Gesetz betreffend die Gesellschaft mit beschränkter Haftung (GmbH-Gesetz). Vol. I: Systematische Darstellungen. §§ 1-34 GmbHG. 2nd, revised ed. München.

Müller 1998 Klaus Müller: Kommentar zum Gesetz betreffend die Erwerbs- und Wirtschaftsgenossenschaften. Vol. III. (§§ 43 – 64c). Bielefeld.

Neumayer 1956 Fritz Neumayer: Vorwort. In: Bundesjustizministerium (Hrsg.): Zur Reform des Genossenschaftsrecht. Referate und Materialien. Vol. I. Bonn.

Parisius 1868 Ludolf Parisius (ed.): Das Preußische Gesetz betreffend die privatrechtliche Stellung der Erwerbs- und Wirthschaftsgenossenschaften vom 27. März 1867 nebst den Einführungs-Verordnungen vom 12. Juli, 12. August und 22. September 1867 und den Ministerial-Instruktionen vom 2. Mai, 10. August, 25. September und 26. Oktober 1867. Mit Einleitung und Erläuterungen zum praktischen Gebrauch für Juristen und Genossenschafter. Berlin.

Parisius 1889 Ludolf Parisius: Das Reichsgesetz, betreffend die Erwerbs- und Wirthschafts-Genossenschaften. Vom 10. Mai 1889. Text-Ausgabe mit Anmerkungen und Sachregister. 2nd extended ed. 11 July 1889. Berlin.

Paulick 1951 Heinz Paulick: Die Stellung der Prüfungsverbände im deutschen Genossenschaftsrecht. In: Zeitschrift für das gesamt Genossenschaftswesen. Vol. I 1951 Issue 3/4.

Pramann 1972 Götz Pramann: Die genossenschaftlichen Betreuungsverbände. Ein Beitrag zur Rechtsstellung der genossenschaftlichen Verbände. Hamburg.

Preußischer LT 1863 Stenographische Berichte. Haus der Abgeordneten [Preußischer Landtag] Anlagen zu den Verhandlungen des Abgeordnetenhauses. Vol. 3, Aktenstück No. 72. Berlin.

Reichskanzlei-Akten 2008 Hans Günter Hockerts and Hartmut Weber (eds.): Akten der Reichskanzlei. Regierung Hitler 1933-1945. Vol. V 1938 Munich. Revised by Friedrich Hartmannsgruber.

RT 1888 Stenographische Berichte über die Verhandlungen des Reichstages. 7. Legislaturperiode – IV. Session 1888/89. Vol. 1. Bd. Berlin. 14th Session on 13 December 1888.

Schröder 1951 Georg Schröder: Der Stand der Reformbestrebungen auf dem Gebiet des deutschen Genossenschaftsrechts. In: In: Zeitschrift für das gesamt Genossenschaftswesen. Vol. I 1951 Issue 3/4.

Schulze 1983 Hagen Schulze: Weimar. Deutschland 1917 – 1933. 2nd, revised ed. Berlin.

Schulze-Delitzsch 1870a Hermann Schulze-Delitzsch: Erster Gesetzentwurf des Verfassers. (Innung der Zukunft Jahrg.

1860 S. 45.). In: Die Entwickelung des Genossenschaftswesens in Deutschland. Auszug aus dem Organ des Allgemeinen Verbandes deutscher Erwerbs- und Wirthschaftsgenossenschaften „Blätter für Genossenschaftswesen" (früher Innung der Zukunft). Berlin.

Schulze-Delitzsch 1870b Hermann Schulze-Delitzsch: Zweiter Gesetz-Entwurf des Verfassers. Das allgemeine deutsche Handelsgesetzbuch und die deutschen Genossenschaften. (Innung der Zukunft 1862, p. 1). In: Die Entwickelung des Genossenschaftswesens in Deutschland. Auszug aus dem Organ des Allgemeinen Verbandes deutscher Erwerbs- und Wirthschaftsgenossenschaften „Blätter für Genossenschaftswesen" (früher Innung der Zukunft). Berlin.

Schulze-Delitzsch 1870c Hermann Schulze-Delitzsch: Die Entwickelung des Genossenschaftswesens. Auszug aus dem Organ des Allgemeinen Verbandes deutscher Erwerbs- und Wirthschaftsgenossenschaften: „Blätter für Genossenschaftswesen" (früher Innung der Zukunft). Berlin.

Schulze-Delitzsch 1883a Hermann Schulze-Delitzsch: Material zur Revision des Genossenschafts-Gesetzes. Nach dem neuesten Stand der Frage geordnet. Leipzig.

Schulze-Delitzsch 1883b Hermann Schulze-Delitzsch: Das socialpolitische Testament [Überschrift der Redaktion]. In: Der Gewerkverein. Organ des Verbandes der Deutschen Gewerkvereine sowie für Einigungsämter, Versicherungs- und Produktivgenossenschaften. 15. Jg.

Seifert 2013 Alexandra Seifert: Über den Tellerrand. Chancen der Rechtsform der „Kleinen Genossenschaft". Die Insolvenzneigung italienischer Genossenschaften. Published. by Heinrich-Kaufmann-Stiftung. Norderstedt Hamburg.

Stappel 2013 Michael Stappel: Die deutschen Genossenschaften 2013. Entwicklungen – Meinungen –Zahlen. Wiesbaden.

St. Jb. 1929 Statistisches Reichsamt (ed.): Statistisches Jahrbuch für das Deutsche Reich. 48. Jg. Berlin.

St. Jb. 1930 Statistisches Reichsamt (ed.): Statistisches Jahrbuch für das Deutsche Reich. 49. Jg. Berlin.

St. Jb. 1931 Statistisches Reichsamt (ed.): Statistisches Jahrbuch für das Deutsche Reich. 50. Jg. Berlin.

St. Jb. 1932 Statistisches Reichsamt (ed.): Statistisches Jahrbuch für das Deutsche Reich. 51. Jg. Berlin.

St. Jb. 1933 Statistisches Reichsamt (ed.): Statistisches Jahrbuch für das Deutsche Reich. 52. Jg. Berlin.

St. Jb. 1940 Statistisches Reichsamt (ed.): Statistisches Jahrbuch für das Deutsche Reich. 58. Jg. Berlin.

Strub 1938 H. B. Strub: Die ländlichen Genossenschaften nach der nationalsozialistischen Erhebung. In: Reinhold Henzler (wiss. Bearbeiter): F. Wilhelm Raiffeisen zum Gedächtnis. Neuwied.

ten Haaf 2006 Hermann-Josef ten Haaf: Kreditgenossenschaften im „Dritten Reich". Bankwirtschaftliche Selbsthilfe und demokratische Selbstverwaltung in der Diktatur (Stuttgarter historische Studien zur Landes- und Wirtschaftsgeschichte 16). Ostfildern.

Thorwart 1889 Friedrich Thorwart: Genossenschaft oder Aktiengesellschaft? In: Blätter für das Genossenschaftswesen (Innung der Zukunft XXXIII. Jg.) Organ des Allgemeinen Verbandes deutscher Erwerbs- und Wirthschaftsgenossenschaften.

Thorwart 1913 Friedrich Thorwart (ed.): Hermann Schulze-Delitzsch's Schriften und Reden. Vol. V. Berlin. (Vol. V, no extra title, incl. biography of Schulze-Delitzsch, acc. preamble the authors are Thorwart and Stein).

Tillmann 1980 Hugo Tillmann: Genossenschaftsgeschichte. In: Eduard Mändle und Hans-Werner Winter (ed.): Handwörterbuch des Genossenschaftswesens. Published for Deutscher Genossenschafts- und Raiffeisenverband e.V. Wiesbaden.

Wehler 2003 Hans-Ulrich Wehler: Deutsche Gesellschaftsgeschichte. Vol. 4. Vom Beginn des Ersten Weltkriegs bis zur Gründung der beiden deutschen Staaten 1914 – 1949. Frankfurt am Main, Zurich, Vienna.

WP-Verordnung 1936 Verordnung über öffentlich bestellte Wirtschaftsprüfer im Genossenschaftswesen. 7 July 1936. Reichsgesetzblatt I, 1936 No. 67.